Resawed Fables

Douglas Malloch

Copyright © BiblioLife, LLC

This book represents a historical reproduction of a work originally published before 1923 that is part of a unique project which provides opportunities for readers, educators and researchers by bringing hard-to-find original publications back into print at reasonable prices. Because this and other works are culturally important, we have made them available as part of our commitment to protecting, preserving and promoting the world's literature. These books are in the "public domain" and were digitized and made available in cooperation with libraries, archives, and open source initiatives around the world dedicated to this important mission.

We believe that when we undertake the difficult task of re-creating these works as attractive, readable and affordable books, we further the goal of sharing these works with a global audience, and preserving a vanishing wealth of human knowledge.

Many historical books were originally published in small fonts, which can make them very difficult to read. Accordingly, in order to improve the reading experience of these books, we have created "enlarged print" versions of our books. Because of font size variation in the original books, some of these may not technically qualify as "large print" books, as that term is generally defined; however, we believe these versions provide an overall improved reading experience for many.

DOUGLAS MALLOCH

RESAWED FABLES

BY
DOUGLAS MALLOCH

———

1911:
AMERICAN LUMBERMAN
CHICAGO

DEDICATION:

TO MY SON, DONALD HERBERT MALLOCH,
WHO CAN'T READ YET,
AND TO ANY OTHERS WHO WILL.

RESAWED FABLES

Of Developing a Specialty

Any High-Brow Farmer will allow that it is difficult to find a General Purpose Cow. Some of our Agricultural Customers will say a Holstein is, and some will say Some Other Critter. This Subject has been debated at every Social Function in Posey County for years, but it is likely to remain Unanswered until T. Roosevelt takes to dairying.

The General Purpose Lumberman is Analogous, whatever that is. It is pretty hard for a Bovine to make good Suet and be a Good Butter Cow also, especially if her Qualities as Beef are tested First. The Best Butter and Beef Cow the Writer ever saw was one of the Gentleman Variety, which Butted its Owner over into the next Quarter Section and was converted into Prime Beef shortly thereafter.

The General Purpose Lumberman is Analogous. It is difficult for a man to be a good Mill Man, a good Timber Buyer, a good Salesman, a good Collector and a good Christian all at one and the same Time. Once there was a Wholesale Lumber Dealer who employed one of these General Purpose Lumbermen. This Man looked after the Buying, the Selling and the Credit Department; and this Trio of Triplets kept him about as busy as Triplets will. Once in a while a Chance to close a Snap on some Log Run slipped through his mitts. Now and then a Sale was not closed up in time because he didn't have the Time with which to close it up. Occasionally a Retail Dealer exploded with a Dull Roar and left the Wholesale Yard Holding the Bag, because the General Purpose Lumberman had not been as Hep to the Retailer's Responsibility as he might have been.

These things Irked both the Wholesaler and the General Purpose Lumberman. The Inevitable happened. It was one of those Cases where a Man was Fired and Quit at the Same Time. Now the Wholesaler has three Men to Wrastle what used to be done by one General Purpose Lumberman. It costs him nearly three times as Much, but he is better Satisfied. As for the General Purpose Lumberman, he is better satisfied also. He is doing Nothing but Buying now for another Wholesale Concern and he is cashing Three Times the Salary he was when holding down Three Jobs—and getting Longer Vacations.

Moral—This is the Age of the Specialist; the

Successful Man is the one who can do one Thing better than Anybody else—or can make People Think he can.

Of Going Up Against the Wrong Proposition

There was Once—only once—a Traveling Salesman for a Belt Factory who had a cute curly Moustache, a Red Vest and a Manner that he thought made Chesterfield look like a Hod Carrier. He generally let the Black Moustache get in its Work first, then he Turned On the Vest (he should have been Pinched for wearing it inside the Fire Limits), and finally let the Winning Manner do the Rest. He believed as a Lady-Killer he had Bluebeard sparring for wind.

One day this Half-Baked Lad, who thought his name ought to be spelled Winner with a Big W, dropped into a Strange Burg to sell a Little Bill of Belts to the R. U. Good Lumber Company. As luck—which was always coming his Way in large sized Packages—would have it, there was no One in the Office when the Heart Smasher strode in in all his Glory but a

Defenseless Woman engaged in looking over the Books—(at about $20 per mo, thought the Wise Guy with the Belt Line). He at once got his Moustache and his Sunset Vest and his Triple-Plate Cheek to work to win her out.

The Rest of the Particulars are Missing and also seven Links of the Belt Salesman's Watch-chain and the Order he was to have gotten from the R. U. Good Lumber Company. Some of the Mill Hands found him in an Inverted Position in a Barrel of Black Grease at the Back of the Office which, while it may have oiled his Moustache, did not improve the Vest. He had to own up that he had tried to Win Out the Female Bookkeeper in the Office and had run up against a Lady Zbyszko in Disguise.

Then One of the Volunteer Life-Saving Crew who had pulled him out of the Grease Barrel had a Happy Thought.

"Why," he ejaculated, "I know who it was you Met."

"I don't care Who it was I met," said the Salesman, "May we never Meet Again. But who was It?"

"That was the Widow Good, the Head of the Company."

Moral—Sometimes When you tackle a Woman You tackle the Wrong Man.

Of Yielding to Temptation

Now it so Happened, as such Things will, that a certain Saw Mill Man in Pennsylvania had three Sons. Two of the Sons were good Sons but the other Son was a Black Sheep. When a mere child the Black Sheep licked the two good Sons singly and syndicated; but be it also said to the Credit of the Black Sheep that he also punched the Everlasting Dickens out of a Brace of School Bullies who tried to hand it to the Good Sons. If there was a Fight or an Expedition to some Farmer's Melon Patch or any Mischief brewing the Black Sheep was Johnny on the Spot. If there was Anything doing in the Trouble Line Black Sheep wanted to be right there when the Trouble was handed out. But the two good Boys were home studying their Trigonometry, whatever that is.

The Three Graces worried through School and went to College, with a Result that might have been expected. The two good Sons got through Astrology and Bugology and came out with the Degree of B. A. The Black Sheep, while he did not get through Trigonometry and Deuteronomy and such Branches, did manage to get through about $120 of the old man's Money every Month and graduated in the Middle of his sophomore Year with the Degree of B. A. A.—which stands for baa, baa, Black Sheep, and is a Degree one Degree higher than the Boiling Point.

Now the wonderful Part of this Story is that the old man never lost confidence in the Black Sheep. He had to admit in the first Place that the Boy had enough Energy to keep him busy getting him out of Scrapes, but he never observed the good Boys burning up Anything around in their Part of the Grounds. He said he would rather see a Man make an Error now and then in the Game of Life than see him loaf and let Easy Outs go by for Base Hits. The Boy's Mother kicked sometimes but the old man sprung the Sowing-His-Wild-Oats Gag on her on these Occasions and managed to keep Peace and the Black Sheep in the Family.

"If he gets through this Time of Life without breaking his Neck or his Father," the Boy's Dad used to say, "he'll be in Shape to appreciate what he's Up Against when he breaks into the Lumber Business. Not that I recommend this Course of Study for any young Man; but Deviltry is like Measles—if a Person is bound to have it Some Time he had better have it while he's Young."

When the Boys had all got Home from College the old man decided to set them up in

Business. So he established three retail Lumber Yards in Towns far enough apart to keep the three Brothers from fighting for Barn Bills as they used to fight for Megs in Boyhood Days. The Governor was tempted to put them all in the same Burg and let the best Man win; but, for the Sake of Peace and Profits, he wisely decided upon the other Course.

Now it came to pass that the first good Son did not do enough Business to keep up his fire Insurance premiums. There may have been Something the Matter with his Town or his Trigonometry. There were some People who said he lacked Practical Experience, while there were Others who came right out in Meeting and declared that all he lacked was Brains.

As might have been expected in a Yarn of this Kind, the Black Sheep did all Kinds of Business at his Yard. When he got a Lumber Yard on his Shoulders he sort of Settled Down, which almost any Man would do under the same Circumstances. At the End of the Year he turned $3,800 over to the Governor as the Proceeds of the Yard its first Season.

The other Son did even better, strange to say. There may have been some Luck in it or it may have been the Bugology that helped him. At any rate, at the End of the Year the Books of the second good Son showed $5,247.63 to the

Credit of the Old Man who had given him the Yard to Boss.

But the Good Young Man couldn't stand the Pressure, and the old man has never cashed in his Credit for $5,247.63. He has blown in pretty near that much for Ads in the Personal Columns stating that if Reginald will return all will be forgiven.

Moral—He is unlucky whose First Temptation is a Big One.

Of Socrates and the Man from Wisconsin

This Fable is for the uplift of the Human Tank who is inclined to cast his lamps on the Wine when it is Red.

This man—an Exception—was a Hemlock Manufacturer at Somewhere, Wis. He had been reading the Sad Fate of one Socrates, who Flourished between 469 and 399 B. C. It bothered him Some to see how a Man could be born in 469 and Die in 399. According to that he had Died Seventy years before he was Born— a Very sad thing to Happen to Any man. However, it is that Way in the books and it might Easily have happened in Some Towns.

Socrates was a Philosopher, like B. A. Johnson and Frank McMillan. He was the Son of Sopronicus, and a pupil of Sumothercus, who taught him to be a Sculptor. Soc thought that rather than be a Sculptor he would be a Philosopher. Sculpting too closely resembled Work, while it was a Snap to philos.

History records that Socrates had a Shrewish Wife, but that he also had a Robust Constitution—which was Well. It is recorded that Socrates once Stood still for twenty-four Hours Entranced in Thought. He was Probably trying to Remember what his Wife Tied the White String on his Finger for.

In 399 Socrates was Charged with Neglecting the Gods of the State and Introducing new Divinities and with Corrupting the Morals of the Young. It is Supposed that this was the Result of his Attempt to Hold a Concatenation.

Similar Charges had been Made twenty-four Years before; but Socrates had a Pull and knew Something about getting Continuances, Writs of Habeas Corpus etc., etc. In his Defense Socrates pointed with Pride to his Past. (A man always has more Confidence in his Past than other People have.) Socrates was Convicted by six Votes out of a possible 500, but expressed a Willingness to submit to a Recount in one or two Doubtful Precincts. The Punishment had still to be Picked Out. Socrates himself Declared that if he were Treated according to his public Services he would be Maintained at Public expense. This provoked the Jury, and it Condemned him to wear a Tombstone. The Jury gave him Thirty days to settle up his Affairs, and then Compelled him to Drink a Cup of Hemlock. This made Socrates the Original Hemlock Consumer, and caused his Subsequent election as the Patron Saint of the Northern Hemlock & Hardwood Manufacturers' Association.

The Hemlock Manufacturer at Somewhere, Wis., mentioned earlier in the Chapter, had been Reading about Socrates and the Hemlock he Consumed, and Wisely decided that where Socrates made his Mistake in Drinking Hemlock was in being too abrupt about it. This man had a Hemlock mill and a few million feet of Hemlock Lumber in stock and a few Million more of Hemlock in the Tree. Instead of Absorbing this in the Rough, and thus filling his System full of Methylconine, he Converted his Hemlock Lumber Yard, his Hemlock mill and his Hemlock Timber into Gin Fizzes, Brandy Sours and the Stuff that made Louisville Famous.

He may have Thought that he had More Fun than Socrates, but he Suffered longer and the Result was the same.

Moral—No man was ever made Rich by Booze, not the Fellow in Front.

Of Piling It On

There are a Lot of Men in this Vale of Tears who have a Good Thing and don't appreciate the Fact. At least that is what their Wives are always Telling them. No one appreciates a Good Thing like a Woman—and no one uses a Mirror as Much.

Once upon a Time there was a Retail Lumber Dealer like that. He was doing a Business like a Lemonade Seller at a Newsboys' Picnic and stood a chance of getting almost as wealthy. It was the Kind of Wealth that comes to a Man slowly but surely—like an Appetite for Olives. But this Man had the Idea he wanted to get Wealthy by Jerks.

So he began to "Enlarge his Business." That's what he Called It. Now, enlarging one's Business is All Right; but that is like a Fellow's Portrait—he doesn't want to enlarge it too large or it will make the Mole on his Face look like the Biggest thing on the Farm, and his Wrinkled Brow like a Corrugated Roof.

It is a Commercial Truth that Good Credit is of Absolutely no Value to a Man unless he uses it. But it is like Congratulations at a Wedding—don't overdo it or in Time the Other Fellow will find out what an Awful Liar you are.

This Man began to use his Credit—a little at first, a lot at last. His Credit was A1, for everybody knew he was simply coining Money. He had a Retail Lumber Business that was a Cinch. He had the People with him. So when he wanted a little money the bank advanced it to him. He told the Bank that it was to enlarge his Business, and the Directors rubbed their Hands and were glad. The local paper told about the Big Stock he was going to put in and printed a Picture of him that represented him in an advanced Stage of Smallpox.

It wasn't so very awful Long before the Thing got to be a Mania with him. He had Dreams at Night and Schemes by Day. After a while the Bank made him get an Indorser. Then he applied to his Friends. At first they were Delighted. After a little While instead of being Delighted they were Busy or Out of Town. It was about this Time that a Coincidence happened. A Coincidence is when two

Things unexpectedly happen at the Same Time —for instance, Twins.

One Day in the merry Month of May the Dealer heard a Crash out in the Yard. At first he thought it might be the Bookkeeper's new Summer Suit, but he determined to Investigate. When he reached the Point of Investigation he found the Hands pulling about 75,000 feet of 2x10x12 off of Mike Malone, the best Lumber Piler in the Business. When they got Mike out he looked like the Busy Part of a Railroad Collision.

"You see it was like This," explained the Yard Foreman. "Mike got swelled on himself. He is a Crackerjack at Standing up Lumber and he knows it. This two-by-ten piles nice and Mike said he would stack up a Lumber Pile that would make the Eiffel Tower look like a Dog House. He'd got it up where it was the Highest Pile of Lumber ever seen in this District; but that wasn't enough. He said it would stand another Course and he went to put it on. It was one Course too much. Mike and the Top of the Pile both started for the ground at the Same Time—but Mike got here First.

"The Wind would have Took the Pile over Anyway before long, so we're Nothing Out. But I feel kind of Sorry for Mike. He'll have to take Some one home with him to Identify him to his wife. It shows that a Man don't want to pile it on Too Thick."

The Lumberman went back to the Office and figured up what Paper he had Floating. Then he tore up a Blank Note and a Mortgage.

Moral—It Doesn't have to be Pointed out; it's Plain Enough.

Of the Man Who Welches

A Traveling Salesman for a Toothpick Factory, a Man who appreciated a Good point whether it was on a Toothpick or in a Story, fell in with a Stranger in the Smoker and invited him into a little, quiet Game of Draw. The Stranger Fell for the Suggestion with celerity. A Couple of other Fellow Passengers were drawn into the Gentlemen's Game and, as no Particular Limit but the End of the Road had been Mentioned, the Jackpots soon became nearly as large as the Purses hung up at the Somerville (N. J.) County Fair.

After the Game had progressed for a Brief Interval there occurred one of those Striking Coincidences that Sometimes happen in Draw Poker—two Men held Combinations which they knew couldn't be Beat if they were Lucky enough to Fill. When the Stranger Fingered over his Pasteboards he found three beautiful Aces, a Six of Hearts and a Seven of Spades. The Toothpick Drummer found three little Trays that looked Pretty Good to him, so·Good in fact that he quietly remarked, "Gentlemen, it'll cost you Ten to draw Cards."

While there was a very comfortable John Pot, the Outsiders could not see Ten Dollars' Worth of Cards in their Hands and promptly backed up. It was now up to the Stranger and he came in with promptitude. On the Draw he was rather Glad he came, for he exchanged his Six and Seven for a Pair of Ladies. The Toothpick Drummer also drew two Cards but he did not get a Pair. Nevertheless he bid Ten Simoleons and the Stranger came back at him with Fifty Better. The Toothpick Agent fingered his Cards again thoughtfully and cautiously, reached into his Pocket and pulled out a Small Wallet and laid down a Hundred.

The two spectators looked at One Another and drew a Little Closer. The Stranger went into a Fit. He grew Red, White and Blue by Turns. He gazed at his three little Aces and his Pair of Queens. They did not look as Big as they had a few minutes ago, but still they looked Pretty Big. The Silence felt like an Ulcerated Tooth.

"It'll cost you Fifty to see what I've got," murmured the man with the Line of Toothpicks.

The Stranger awoke with a Start. Then he also Dove down into his Inner Compartments and pulled out a Black, religious-looking Wallet. From its recesses he plucked two Twenties and a Ten. The Toothpick Man laid down Four Trays.

The Cards dropped from the Stranger's hands and the Toothpick Drummer began folding up the greenbacks. Then the Stranger spoke in the Voice of a man opening a Memorial Meeting.

"Are you really going to take it?" he asked.

"Why not?" asked the Toothpick man, pausing in surprise.

"Because when I played that fifty Dollars I risked more than the Money; I Risked my Reputation and my Sacred Honor. That was the Firm's Money."

"Yes, you risked it and I won it and it's Mine. But, Stranger," said the Toothpick man, passing Fifty Dollars back to the other man, "I'll stake you back to your Reputation and your Sacred Honor and ask you this One Question: Would your Sacred Honor have been O. K. if you had Won?"

Moral—We never Recognize the Wickedness of the Game until we Lose.

Of Keeping the Faith

Once upon a Time there was a bunch of saw mill men who were sawing lumber to beat the Band. But the Band came up again serenely every morning and asked for More. The Amount of this particular lumber that these unparticular lumbermen were sending out upon a cold, unfeeling world was, however, away out of proportion to the Financial Returns that Blew in in the Daily Mail. The mill men were apparently making lumber for their Health, but this was not having the Tonic Effect that might be Expected. They decided finally to hold a Medical Congress and see if the Trouble lay in the netherschorosis or in the supercerebrum.

This consultation, or ante-mortem investigation, was the result of the Enterprise and Postage of I. Sawyer Wood, who had Dared the Bunch to Sit down Together at the Hotel de Bumjoint. Mr. Wood looked over the list of the Men engaged in this line of Sawdust Manufacture and bagged 89 out of a possible 93, giving him an average of .957. When the Sawmillers had Coagulated Somewhat, Mr. Wood made a Proposition that they put the Business where it would yield Dividends instead of Headaches.

He proposed to do this by shutting down all the Mills from 3:07 to 3:24 p. m. every Thursday.

Most of those present expressed a Hearty Willingness to subscribe to the Agreement, but some of the Bashful Ones were disposed to Hang Back. They were worried about the Other Four who were not at the Meeting. Had it been a meeting to Whack Up Something the absence of the Terrible Four would not have Worried them so much.

But the more the Among Those Present considered the Absent Ones the More Were they Persuaded that until the Fearful Four came into the Fold there could be Nothing Doing.

I. Sawyer Wood sidestepped a Talkfest and calmed their Fears by agreeing Personally to make a Junket to Diagnose the Cases of the Absent Ones. Thereupon he succeeded in getting those present to Subscribe to an Instrument that was expected to Blow Holes in the Cloud of Financial Depression and bring on a Shower of Gold Shekels. Then the Meeting adjourned, subject to the Call of the Janitor.

Two weeks later I. Sawyer Wood started out to see what Ailed the Four Foolish Virgins. He found that one Sawmiller had contracted his Season's cut and to Limit it might involve a Lawsuit. The next man had some Notes coming Due and by keeping up his Gait he was just able to look the Bank Cashier in the Face. The Third Man was working on a Special Bill and he had to Go Some to get it out according to Schedule. The Fourth Man explained that he didn't make his Glad Presence known at the Meeting because he had been Sawmilling so long under present conditions that he didn't have the Price.

All would have been well if I. Sawyer Wood had not Continued his Travels. He went eleven miles up the railroad; and then he Realized with a Great Throb of Sadness that he had gone Too Far. He ran into the Saw Mill of one of the Fellows who had signed the compact. It was 3:15 p. m. Thursday and the old Mill was buzzing away as though there wasn't an Agreement within 17,000 miles. I. Sawyer Wood stalked up to the Office, but it had little Effect on the Sawmill man, although I. Sawyer Wood is not such a Bum Stalker at that. The Mill Man explanationed why he had broken the Compact. His Wife's Folks had just come to Spend the Winter and he needed the Money.

Our Hero now decided that it was up to him to do a little more Hawkshaw business. At the fatal 17 minutes of the next fatal Thursday he found another Mill Chewing away like a stenographer with the Pepsin habit. This man explained that he was afraid if he shut down for 17 minutes once a Week the steam would Chill and give the boilers Pneumonia.

The next Offender I. Sawyer discovered said he was compelled to run in order to get Sawdust to burn to make more Sawdust to Burn to make more Sawdust.

The worst was yet to come. At last I. Sawyer stumbled on a man who was running Overtime in order to stock up for the Rise. The Man had been the Main Spieler of the Bunch that Raved about the Absent Four.

Moral—Look out for the man who worries about the good Faith of the Other Fellow.

Of the Moving of Lumber in Kansas

A Lawsuit is something which catches a Man when he's down and finishes up the Job. Sliverson Notts, who operated a Retail Lumber Yard in Cornville, Kan., feared a Lawsuit like a Hypocrite fears the Truth. Sliverson Notts was up against it Good and Proper. Things hadn't been breaking his Way for some Months and in Endeavoring to Tide over the financial Cyclone Sliverson Notts had been distributing his Paper over his Part of Kansas like the Opposition Car of a Circus. He had been circulating his Autograph in Kansas like a New Member of the United States Senate in Washington after his Maiden Speech.

The Fox chased by Hounds is All Right as long as the Hounds come at him One at a Time and don't all Jump on him at Once. That is the Way it was with Sliverson Notts, of Kansas. So long as the Men who Held his Autograph came at him One at a Time he was Safe; but he feared the Result if one of them should bring Suit and Fetch the Whole Pack down on him together. He realized that an Era of simultaneous Collections would put the Sliverson Notts Lumber Company very much to the Bad.

Things were Coming a little better for Sliverson Notts when one Day he got Wind that some Blamed Fool had begun to Get Worried about his Money and had begun Suit against him. The B. F. knew it would Bust Sliverson Notts up in Business but figured he would be in on the Ground Floor when the Crash came, anyway. As for Sliverson Notts, he knew that Creditors would be Camped around his Lumber Yard in the Morning like Believers at a Free Methodist Camp Meeting. If the B. F. had only left him Alone a Week or so longer he would have come out of it All Right.

Sliverson Notts was informed by an Obliging Friend, who Ran up to Tell him so as to see how he Took it, that the Papers had been drawn up that Afternoon and the Attachment on the Lumber would be Served in the Morning along with his Grape-Nuts. He went to Bed that Night feeling like a Man who is going to do a Dancing Specialty on the Sheriff's Elevated Platform. He Knew it was useless Battling against the inevitable—which is another Name for a Kansas Sheriff.

That Night the wind soughed Dismally about the House, like a Hired Girl with the Toothache. In the Morning Sliverson Notts arose and Wandered down to take a Farewell Look at his Lumber Yard. When he reached the Spot he Rubbed his Eyes with Amazement and a Bandana Handkerchief. The Spot was there All Right but the Lumber Yard, where was It?

There were a few Plank scattered about and these Scattered Plank led off in a Southeasterly Direction. Sliverson Notts followed the Trail. He tramped all Day and at Nightfall, twenty-seven miles from Home, he came upon his Lumber Yard slightly disheveled but laid out just as it had been Laid Out back in Kansas. Now it was in Texas, thanks to a Zephyr which had Picked it up during the Night.

Business was Pretty Good in Texas and

Sliverson Notts was soon rather Glad he Moved. After some months of Prosperity, one Day he journeyed Back to Kansas. The Inevitable Sheriff met him with a Glad Hand and a Body Attachment. But Sliverson Notts drew himself up Proudly. "Stand Back," he said, "I've got coin enough to pay 'em all. I knew I could do it if they Gave me Time."

"When you Going to move Back?" asked the Inevitable.

"You can .Search Me," replied Sliverson Notts. "I'm liable to come Back almost Any Old Time."

Moral—It's an Ill Wind that Blows Nobody Good.

Of Combining Brains and Capital

There were once two Comrades who grew up Side by Each, sharing each Other's Sorrows and sharing each Other's Toys. At School they fought for and with each other, loved the same Girl and used the same Brand of Gum. The Girl was freckled and had a pimple on the Lee side of her Nose. She was, ye Gods, how beautiful, and she was the only Thing that ever came between them. She walked Home from School that Way.

The Comrades used to lie on the River Bank and lie about what they intended to be when they grew up. Down the Stream they could hear the drowsy Hum of the Saw Mill. A Saw Mill always has a drowsy Hum in a Book. In Reality a good, active Saw Mill which is in the Enjoyment of ordinary Health can keep a whole Neighborhood awake if it is running Nights. But "Drowsy Hum" sounds like Harry Miller and so it goes in here out of Compliment to Harry.

As they saw the Saw Mill and heard its drowsy Hum and felt the Ground Tremble when a big Log rolled on to the Log-deck or the Foreman cussed in his accustomed Manner, they were fired with a great Ambition to own a Saw Mill themselves. Eventually they swore a solemn Oath that, Sinker Swim, Liver Die, Survivor Perish, they would butt into the Saw Mill Business. In Time they forgot the freckle faced Girl with the Pimple on her Jibstay but they never surrendered their cherished Ambition to get into the Saw Mill Push.

Dick was the son of rich but honest Parents and when he got older and began to know less they sent him to College where he won such Success he was made a regular Halfback. Jack also went to the Harvard Brain Factory but it was only by Means of hard Scraping by the Old

Man. Jack, in consequence, had less spending Money and more Time for Study. He was not posted on all the fast Horses and Hounds in the Vicinity but he became somewhat acquainted with Caesar and Homer, who are mighty good Fellows even though they are dead. Both boys were graduated with Honors. Jack was Valedictorian and Dick Captain of the Team.

After they had Escaped from College and were again at Large each renewed his Determination to break into the Saw Mill Business. Dick had a Father he could Draw on. The only Thing Jack had to draw on was a Corncob Pipe. The two hopeful Lads started out together to seek their Fortunes in the Saw Mill Business. Dick got hold of a Tract in Roscommon County, Michigan, and decided to cut it. He offered Jack, who had no coin with which to buy standing Pine, a Job as Boss of the Mill. But Jack demurred.

"Dick," he said, "I don't know any more about the Saw Mill Business than you do—and you don't know a Blamed Thing. I don't know an Edger from an Elevator—and you know the Same. I think it is up to us to assimilate some Experience and I refuse to assimilate mine at your Expense. I've been doing that with your Cocktails but darned if I will with your Experience."

The Reader will see why Jack was made the Valedictorian of his Class, when he could Orate like that. Dick tried to prevail upon him to change his Mind, but he might as well have talked to a Woman. Jack told him there were Men driving Dumpcarts who knew more about the Business than he did. As for himself, he was going to try it Alone. Thus the Comrades parted.

Dick Built a Mill. He had to depend upon practical Saw Mill Men and Father's Bank Account a good deal. Finally he got the Thing started and hired a Chap to run it and send him Monthly Reports. Then Dick went to Detroit, joined a Couple more Clubs, got married and did a number of other reckless Things. He had determined to settle down and enjoy Life and the Monthly Reports from his Roscommon County Saw Mill.

Jack went up Country a short Distance. He had three hundred and fifty Plunks with which to go out into the World and make a Million. He invested his Capital in a portable Saw Mill and began custom sawing Railroad Ties for the Grand Rapids & Indiana Railroad. The Mill was a Saw Mill in the fullest Sense, as it possessed but one Saw. It was operated by a threshing Machine Engine blocked outside the Mill. One Day the Farmer's Boy who was first and last Engineer by mistake threw the Traction Attachment on and the Engine pulled the Saw Mill three Rods before it could be stopped. After this pleasant Occurrence Jack ran the Engine himself.

The Reports Dick received down at Detroit were not always encouraging. He decided to change Superintendents, which recalls what Mr. Lincoln said about the Wisdom of swapping Horses when crossing a Stream. Things went from Bad to Worse and Dick went from Detroit to Roscommon County. He finally tried to run the Mill himself and he proved to be the Worst that had tackled the Job yet. Down in Detroit he had learned how to play a Whist Hand to Perfection but not how to handle a Saw Mill Gang or get the most out of a Mill.

Up at the Tie Mill Jack was having a real nice Time. He never knew whether he would be able to look the next Pay Day in the Face or not, and Something was always busting around the Premises—in fact, Everything from the Circular to the Proprietor's Suspenders. Between standing off Employees and Machinery Manufacturers Jack was as busy as a Candidate in a Caucus.

One Day down in Grand Rapids Jack and Dick bumped into each other. They went and enjoyed a Dinner—which to Jack was now an infrequent occurrence—and Mutual Confidences. The next Day the Tie Mill went out of Business, Dick went back to Detroit and Jack found himself with a Bank Account and a fund of Experience to draw on. It is Dick, Jack & Co., and now they are coining Money.

Moral—Many a man with Brains hasn't Brains Enough not to Depend on Brains Alone; Many a man with Money hasn't Money Enough to be in the Saw Mill Business unless he has Brains Enough to Pay Money Enough to Get Brains Enough to Help him Run It.

Of the Value of Directness

The Firm of Greene & Browne—which was not its Real Name at all, but is used merely to give Color to the Story—decided to Plant a Saw Mill in a Tract of Timber on the Squahomish River. Steele & ReSette, who sell Lumber Manufacturing Machinery in Chicago, and the Kerlin Iron Works, engaged in the Same Business in New York, heard about it almost simultaneously. Almost simultaneously Steele & ReSette, of Chicago, and the Kerlin Iron Works, of New York, Wired Two Salesmen as Follows, to-wit, that is to Say:

RESAWED FABLES

CHICAGO, ILL., January 23, 1911.

H. H. HAPP, Portland, Ore.
 See Greene & Brown immediately; in market for mill.
STEELE & ReSETTE.

NEW YORK, N. Y., January 23, 1911.

GABRIEL GITHAR, Greenville, Ga.
 Greene & Browne want to Buy a Sawmill. Get there, Gabriel.
KERLIN IRON WORKS.

Almost simultaneously upon Receipt of these Telegrams the Two Salesmen Wired:

PORTLAND, ORE., January 23, 1911.

GREENE & BROWNE:
 Will call on you with a fine line of Sawmills January 25.
H. H. HAPP.

GREENVILLE, GA., January 23, 1911.

GREENE & BROWNE:
 Don't do Anything until you Hear from Me. Sample Sawmill Gone Forward by Express.
GABRIEL GITHAR.

Almost simultaneously H. H. Happ and Gabriel Githar reached the Office of Greene & Browne, January 26. It was almost simultaneous, but it was Happ who got there First. Happ decided to place his Money on the Greene and was soon in Greene's Private Office. When Githar arrived he also decided to try the Greene, but he found that Handsome Harry already had the Head of the Firm cornered. So Githar had to be content with Browne.

Meanwhile Happ was progressing happily with Greene in the Private Office. He told him a few Funny Stories, made him smoke a Good Cigar, and Talked to him about the Hardwood Outlook, although he didn't know any more about Hardwoods than Michael Angelo did about the Price of Lath. This consumed so much Time that Greene told Happ he had better come around at 3 p. m. if he wished to talk Saw Mill Machinery.

Happ went away very well satisfied with his Morning's Work. "Guess I stand in pretty well with the Old Man now," he said to Himself, Himself being the only Person within Hearing Distance at the Time. When he went back at 3 p. m. Mr. Greene said:

"Guess we won't have to talk that Saw Mill Machinery Matter, after all. I kind of turned that over to Browne, and he closed a Deal this Morning with Githar, of the Kerlin Iron Works."

Moral—The Man who is up to Snuff gets down to Business.

Of the Straw that Dislocated the Camel's Vertebrae

A Bank Cashier whose Health had become critical in the eastern Burg in which he handled the Germ-infected but none the less desirable Coin of the Realm decided to locate under the sunny Skies of Colorado. He had concluded that a Change of Scene would do him Good. The Village Doctor told him so and, as the Village Doctor was also the President of the Bank, the Cashier felt constrained to take his Advice. He took not only the Doctor's Advice but $1,800 that the Doctor had accumulated giving Advice to other Patients.

When the Cashier struck Highfive Gulch with his bad Cough and the Doctor's Advice and his Eighteen Hundred done up in a small grip he was one of the tenderest of the tender among Tenderfeet. He had been reading yellow-backed books about the Wild and Hirsute West and when he stepped off the Train at the Depot he expected to be shot on his first Appearance or on the Foot or Somewhere. However, no one took a Crack at him, and, as a Matter of Fact, no one even observed him get off the Choo-Choo Cars.

This somewhat Disappointed the Man from the effete East, and he went over to Blur-Eyed Dick's Trouble Factory and filled up on some Booze that was warranted to kill at a Hundred Yards. Then he went out looking for Trouble and he found it Outside waiting for him. He met a Man who had a Temper and a Gun that were both Operated with a Hair Trigger.

If this were a Piece of Fiction instead of a Truthful Tale this would be the Place for the Moral to come in. As a Matter of Fact, the Cow Puncher said, "Hello, Doughface," and the Doughface responded in an even more complimentary Manner. Then both began to shoot the Shoots, a popular Amusement at that Period in the West. In a Story the Cashier would have been made to resemble a Sieve. As a Matter of Fact, he bored a Hole in the Gun Fighter at the first Crack out of the Box.

In the eastern Burg from which the Bank Cashier had recently set sail one can not shuffle off some Other Mortal's Coil with Impunity. If you puncture Some One's Anatomy back there —or in front—there is often apt to be an Investigation as to your Provocation. Having been brought up in this Atmosphere, the Bank Cashier knew what to expect. Two Hours later, when a Committee of the Leading Citizens of Highfive Gulch bore down on him, each with a

Gun Barrel looking with its One Eye right at the Bank Cashier, the latter Gentleman had already begun to wonder what particular Tree they would select for him to ornament, when the Chairman spoke. On behalf of the Citizens of Highfive Gulch, the best prospect in the Rockies, he wished to extend to the Stranger the sincere Thanks of the Community for his Efforts in the Way of Public Improvement which had removed from the camp the Orneriest Cuss that ever rode into the town on a stolen Bronc.

This Incident encouraged the Tenderfoot quite a little, and the next Morning, having filled up on Red-eye again, he started out to kill time and a few more of the Inhabitants. But his Reputation had got abroad and the People were as scary as Partridges. The new Terror wandered up the Gulch without finding any Trouble until he came to the tall Timber. Then an Idea struck him; it would have been better for him if it had been a Brick. He thought of a Scheme to start some Excitement. Sure enough he did.

The Bad Man from the east gathered together a few Handfuls of dry Twigs at the Edge of the Timber and set them afire. Then he sat down to watch the Fun. It came sooner than he had expected. As the Flames ate their Way into the Forest the People poured up from the

Gulch. Every Man of them had a Bucket in his hand save one. He had a Rope.

Moral—You can grow a Man in Twenty Years, but it takes a Hundred to make a Tree.

Of the Lumbermen's Derby

A Colt that was taken out of a Pasture and put into Harness for the First Time concluded it was up to him to Surprise the Sporting Writers with a New Mark on a Mile Track. He was out of a Stable that had never Worked out any 2:05 Hosses, but had produced a few Trotters that were a Good Bet in the Race of Life on a Cold Day and a Heavy Track. His Sire was a grand old Mud Horse who ran Against Adversity and Panic in the Great 1893 Handicap and distanced a Field of Starters that Looked like Sure Winners before the Official Handicapper, Hard Times, Got in his Work. But this New Colt with the Fancy Training, and the Fine Grooming that his Father had not been Lucky enough to Enjoy, decided to Set a Mark for the Family. Give him a Good Track and No Breeze and he knew he could clip Ten Seconds off the Old Man's Time and make him look like a Selling Plater.

The Owner was willing to give the Colt a Chance, so he Started him in the Lumbermen's Derby. The Entrance Fee was about $10,000, which was Cheerfully Paid, and $5,000 more was expended for a Stable at one of the Big Tracks where they run off the Lumbermen's Derby, no matter what the Track or Weather. There was a Bunch of Other Entries, including Long Experience, Hard Work, Wise Estimator and Other Horses which had taken a Share of the Purses every Year in the Lumbermen's Derby. The Colt with the Fancy Stable and the Good Backing was sure there would be Nothing to it when it came to a Race with these Oldtime Slowcoaches.

They got away in a Bunch and the Colt Simply ran away from the Field for the Eighth and the Quarter. Then Long Experience began to Close up the Gap and they ran Neck and Neck in the Stretch Turn with Hard Work at their Heels on the Back Stretch running easy, and keeping his Wind and looking like a Strong Finisher to Oldtimers in the Stand.

Then Something Happened. The Colt, crowded for the Pole when he Expected to Canter in, broke and went up in the Air at the Turn, and Hard Work was by him in a Twinkling. It was now a Grand Race between Long Experience and Hard Work, with Long Experience holding a Good Lead. But in the Stretch Hard Work showed his Going Powers. He buckled down and Beat Long Experience to the Wire by a Length, while Wise Estimator Captured Third Money. As for the Colt, he got the Flag.

Moral—In the Race for Commercial Supremacy, Hard Work is a Better Proposition than a Fancy Hoss with a Monogram on his Blanket and a Green Rider up.

Of the Lumberman By Proxy

There are a few Chaps in this Land of the Free and Home of the Street Car Companies who are Lumbermen by Proxy. They are Scattered around the Country like Men at a Thursday night Prayer Meeting; but occasionally the Traveling Man runs into them and detects them Immediately. He may not have enough Detective Ability to spot Balls in a Pool Room, but the Traveling Man can pick out the Proxy Lumberman like a Colored Poultry Fancier finding the Fattest Pullet on a dark and stormy Night.

The Lumberman by Proxy, however, is Deadly in Earnest. He thinks he is the Real Thing —free from Shake and as Clear as a legal Decision. He imagines he is Carrying all the Brains of the Establishment around under his Fedora, when, as a Matter of Fact, they are Distributed around More or Less among Other People. He doesn't Know that there are a Lot of Men working for him who know that He doesn't know that They know that He doesn't know a lot of things that They know that He doesn't know.

This is one Type of the Lumberman by Proxy. There is Another Type who takes himself in Earnest, but who considers his Opportunity even more Earnestly. He knows that there are Men in his employ who know more about Skidding Logs or Scaling Logs or Skinning Prices than he does; but he doesn't overlook the Fact that that isn't necessarily all. He knows that a Ship may have its Rigging full of good Sailors, but go on the Rocks unless there is a good Man at the Wheel.

Once upon a Time there was a Lumberman by Proxy of the Latter Class who had good Men to boss the Jobs that he couldn't boss himself. They got along as smoothly as a Ladies' Whist Club for a considerable Period of Time. Then one day one of the Men got Gay and jumped his Job. He expected to see the Proxy Lumberman go fifty-seven feet into the air and explode like a Toy Balloon; but the Foxy Proxy Lumberman had been standing by All the Time; and the Man who jumped found that the Man who six

Months ago knew absolutely Nothing about his Particular Specialty could now do it better than the Jumper could himself.

About two More jumped and then felt a Good Deal like a Yearling Heifer that jumps over a Field Fence into a Road Ditch and finds it can't get back. There was in Each Case a good Man to take the Place of Each until Some One Else could be found; and the good Man in Each Case was the Boss.

Moral—The Less a Man thinks he Knows, the More he is Likely to Learn.

Of Troubles

A Saw Mill Man who was Trying to Do Some Figuring was Annoyed by b. (Key to this Joke —Annoyed by a Small Bee.) He took a Soak at It when It Lit on his Left Ear and It Transferred Its Attentions to His Right. It Alighted on his Nose and was Otherwise Over-Familiar. Finally it Stuck its Proboscis into the Back of his Neck up to the Hilt. Then the Saw Mill Man Arose and Swore Blue Blazes.

That Same Night his Mill Burned up and his Yard Burned Down and Ten years of his Life Went up in smoke, but he Didn't Say a Word.

Moral—It is the Little Troubles that Make Men Cuss; the Big Troubles They Rather Expect.

Of the School of Experience

A Youth who had Read in his Copy Book at the District School that Virtue is its own Reward, and a Few other Choice Spencerian Mottoes, and who was as Independent as the Standard Oil Company, bearded the Old Man in his Den one Balmy November Evening and Spoke thus, that is to Say:

"Pa, I want you to Send me to College."

Now, Pa had about as much Experience with Colleges as a Zulu has had shoveling Snow, and he thinks a College Education is about as Essential as a Snow Shovel down in Sunny Africah. The Boy knew his Parent's Opinion on the Subject, and what to Expect; so he was not Disappointed when Papa Replied:

"Back to Earth, Sonny. I'm not going to make a college Professor out of you. You'd Better take a Couple of Years off to See the World, and then come Back and help the Old Man run this Saw Mill Business."

"Just what I intend to Do, Pa, after I've had Proper Preparation."

"Proper Preparation? Don't I run a pretty good Business?"

"A fine Business."

"Made Some Money, haven't I?"

"I believe So."

"Didn't ever hear of Me being Run through one of these Brain Factories, did you?"

"You never Attended College, I believe."

"Why should you, when I Didn't?"

"Because I can—and you Couldn't."

"You mean you have a Rich Father and I didn't?"

"Perhaps that's It."

"Well, my Boy, I don't want it Said I ever denied you Anything. When you was a Boy you Wanted a Green Apple once. I knew you would Regret it, but I knew you wouldn't Believe me if I told you so. So I let you have it and sent for the Doctor. I know how it will be. In a few years you'll come out of College and the Old Man will have to Hustle Around to make enough to keep up with your Swelled Ideas."

"No, Father; you help me through College, and when I come Out I'll Look after Myself."

"Well, you can go to College, and we'll See."

Four years and the Boy came out of School. He hung around Home a Month and then said he was going out into the World. The Old Man determined to find out how many Pounds

Weight his College Education and his Grit would stand, so he let him go unmolested. The Boy had spent Four Years at Civil Engineering, Mathematics and Commercial Practice. But other men had been through the Same Course and were Holding the Jobs. He started by Applying for a position as Superintendent of Construction of a Railroad, and wound up by taking a Job wheeling Lumber in Beech's Lumber Yard. "There'll Come a Time Some Day," quoth he. "You can't Keep a Good Man Down."

Mr. Beech's Right Bower was a Young Man in whom he Reposed the Utmost Confidence and the Combination of his Safe. Unknown to Mr. Beech, the Right Bower was engaged in a Studious and More or Less Successful Attempt to Euchre him out of Some of his Visible Assets. One Day the Red-Lipped Monster of Suspicion found a Way into Mr. Beech's Generous Triple-Expansion Heart. He decided to Investigate the Books. But how was he to do the Deed? He Might be Mistaken, and he did not want the Right Bower to know. To employ an Accountant would at once excite Suspicion and start the Right Bower on a Trip to Niagara Falls, Ont.

Wending his Way through the Yard One Day without any Idea where he would wend to, he wended into a Lumber Shover who did not look the Part. He engaged him in Conversation.

That Night he and the Lumber Shover sat up Late at the Office. So did Mrs Beech at home, but that was Merely Incidental.

Now, the Lumber Shover is Right Bower. To Mr. Beech? Dear, no!—to the Old Man, who had to Pay him a Bigger Salary than the Big One Beech was paying him to Get him.

Moral—There are a Lot of Men who would make Good Confidential Clerks who are Wheeling Lumber; there are also a Number of Confidential Clerks who would make Passable Lumber Shovers.

Of Patriotism

Once upon a Time there was a man who sought employment in a Lumber Yard. He didn't really have to work, but he preferred Work to going without Food. The Gentle Public hears a good Deal about Art for Art's Sake and the Love of Labor, but if the truth were investigated it would be found that the Desire for three good Meals a Day is responsible for most of the great Songs that are composed and the great literary Masterpieces (see herewith) that are Written.

It was perhaps unfortunate for this Man that he broke into the Profession of Piling Lumber just before July 4, because the great Natal Day was responsible for a Ruction the First Thing. And a Ruction in a Lumber Yard is not always so tame an affair. This particular Lumber Yard was located in a Town that was as full of patriotism as the Butter at a Summer Picnic is of Bugs.

When July 4 precipitated itself upon the waiting World, the Lumber Yard shut up and shut down. If any one had mentioned the word "Work" to a Lumber Shover that day, there would have been Work all right, but it would have been Work for the Undertaker. The Lumber Shovers were going to celebrate, and in Consequence there was considerable doing along Main Street.

About 4 p. m. some one noticed that the Stranger was not Celebrating. He was not with the Boys. He was not firing any Firecrackers. It was said he didn't even have a Flag out. This was an outrage. So a delegation of Citizens went up to his House, full of Indignation—mostly Liquid.

After they had gently remonstrated with the Stranger by tearing down a few rods of Fence and breaking a few Sash Lights, they permitted him to say a Word.

"You see, boys," he said, "I ain't shootin' off many Fireworks, because it would make Mother feel kind of bad. It'd make her think more'n more o' the days when all the Children was

Home an' we used to have such Rip-Roarin' Celebrations on the old Farm down in Pennsylvany. Then I used to put on the old blue Coat that I wore through the Vicksburg Campaign, with the medal that Sherman got for me himself. But now me and Mother is Alone. Mary's a hospital Nurse. Harry's in the Philippines. And the Old Flag we Wrapped around Jack when they brought him Back from Cuba—that's why there ain't no Flag out.''

Moral—Don't judge a man's Patriotism by the Amount of Fireworks or Oratory he shoots off.

Of Baseball and Business

This is the Time of year when a Fellow likes to steal away from a Hot Office and a Noisy Mill out to the Cool and Peace of the Baseball Grounds, where he can Recline on the Upholstered Bleachers and yell himself Hoarse in the Face. He puts off his Dignity and his Collar and Necktie and shouts "Robber" at a man 200 feet Away that he wouldn't stand up Three Rounds with if the Purse were $100,000, Loser take all. It is Wonderful how Brave and Sassy a Man can be under such Circumstances. There's many a Chap who couldn't Lick a Stamp who, when he gets on a Ball Ground, is entitled to the Belt as Champion Long-Distance Fighter of the World.

A Man can not go Anywhere, however, without learning Something, unless it is to the Senate Gallery. He can always pick up a few pointers that are useful to him in his Business—if he has any Business Left at the end of the Season. A man can learn a Lot at a ball Game, particularly if he Bets on some $8,000 pitcher.

There is a Retail Lumber Dealer in Detroit who Fans like a Blower System when the Home Team is in Town. He has attended every Game the home team has played this season and a couple of other Exhibitions that John Shaw didn't call Games at all. But he hasn't been getting all he Paid for at the Gate. He hasn't been acquiring those Moral Lessons to which Reference was made earlier in the Chapter.

This Particular Dealer is one of those two-horsepower Affairs that you occasionally see in the Business. He does the Work all Right, but he never seems to break any Records. He is one of these Worldlings who never make a Failure —and never make a Success big enough to get their Names in the Paper. Ordinarily when he goes to a Ball Game he sits next to a Fat Man who Fans himself with a Noon Edition and makes Profane Remarks about the Weather and the Shortstop.

The other Day, however, when he went to the Game, Chance set him down next to a Real Live Philosopher, without Extra Charge. The Philosopher had been a Player and had once been in a Big League for 4 days, 11 hours and 17 minutes. He had Licked up Knowledge on the Players' Bench, which is the only Place to learn Baseball. There are a lot of Promising Once Wases studying the Game there Now.

The Philosopher was full of Knowledge and he liked to work it off on the Helpless Bleacherites around him. He got his Cue when the Visiting Left Fielder let a Ground Ball through him after a Hard Run. "Back to the Sand Lot!" yelled a man Down in Front.

"That's the Way," quoth the Philosopher. "It's the man who Goes After 'em that Gits the Merry Knock, while the Loafer who lets 'em go by for Base Hits is solid with the Fans. But notice this: The Lads who play Errorless Ball never last long in Fast Company. It's the same in the Game of Life. It's the lad who takes a Chance at scooping a Line Drive or makes a Run for a Pop-up who gets the Managers Fighting for him, even if he makes an Error now and then, and not the Man with the Fancy Fielding Average. In Life, it's the Lad who makes a Mistake now and then, and makes the Things that offset Mistakes, that Dame Fortune keeps on her Claim List."

The Dealer began to wonder if he had been Loafing on Hard Chances because he feared he might get his Name in the Error Column. He concluded he had. So he wrote down in his Mental Notebook this:

Moral—A Man never made a Home Run by waiting for a Base on Balls.

Of the Wisdom of Keeping Moving

A Person from the wild and wooly West, who possessed a Chin Whisker that reminded all who beheld it of Hogan's Goat more than anything else, hit Chicago one Day and steered up to a Place where they sell Saw Mills and other little Trinkets like that. He said he wanted to buy a Saw Mill and so the polite Floorwalker steered him down to the Saw Mill Counter, otherwise the Head Salesman's Desk. The H. S. asked him just what kind of a Saw Mill Outfit he was considering the advisability of purchasing and the Man from Ioway reckoned that a portable Saw Mill would satisfy his Wants about as well as Anything.

The Head Salesman tried to persuade him that a portable Mill was n.g., but that if he desired to purchase a Saw Mill Outfit for more or less permanent location he could sell him a line of Saw Mill Machinery that had taken three Gold Medals at the Swedeburg (Neb.) World's Fair. Oh, no, the Person did not want a portable Mill; what he wanted was one of the Cass Tyrne Machine Company's regulation Outfits.

The Person from Ioway reckoned he knew what he wanted and remarked that he didn't need any sawed-off Sissy to tell him he wanted Something else b' Gosh, nuther. He didn't have the ready Money to pay for the Mill, he knew that, but he had some little Cash he could pay down and he guessed he would be good for the Rest. There didn't have to be any Red-Nosed Runt behind a 2x4 Desk in a 6x8 Office to indicate to him what he wanted, b' Gosh, he said. The Head Salesman heard his remarks and thought that would retain him for the Space of a few Moments. He did venture to remark that he didn't see why it was so absolutely necessary that the Saw Mill should be of the portable Pattern, but if the Ioway Person wanted a portable a portable he should have.

The Ioway Person said that that was none of the Head Salesman's blamed Business. He had come to Chicago after a portable Saw Mill and a Portable Saw Mill he was goin' to git. Now, the Cass Tyrne Machinery Company manufactures a portable Mill that is a Beaut. It is so readily transportable that there is a Burglar Alarm on the Mud Drum to keep Somebody from carrying it away. It did not take the Stubby Head Salesman long to fit that Ioway Person out with a portable Saw Mill when once the Ioway Person had succeeded in impressing it on his gigantic Intellect that it was a portable Mill he was arter. The Ioway Person paid his little Deposit and gave the Cass Tyrne Machine Company his Note for the Rest at six Months.

After the Ioway Person had departed the Head Salesman continued to wonder why it was that he had been bound and determined to have a portable Mill. After the Mill was shipped, however, he ceased to wonder, because he had other Things to wonder at. One never lacks for Things to wonder at in Chicago.

He had quite forgotten the Iowa Person when one Day the Secretary and Treasurer and Head Bookkeeper of the Cass Tyrne Machine Company approached his Cell and asked if he remembered selling a Party out in Iowa a portable Saw Mill at six months. The Head Salesman did. The Sec. and Treas. informed him that seven months had now flown on the wings of Time and the Ioway Person's Note was still unpaid.

Tempus fugit and seemed likely to continue to fugit, but the Coin came not. A Bank out that way had returned the Note with thanks.

The Head Salesman had to make a Trip out to Decorah anyway and he said he would make a Side Trip and jar the Iowa Person up a little. A Week later he was driving across Country to where they said the Ioway Person had his Mill, or rather the Cass Tyrne Machine Company's mill. As he drove along he found that pretty nearly Everybody in that Part of Iowa knew the Ioway Person. He was famous. He was celebrated. If there was Anybody in that Section of the State that the Ioway Person didn't owe, it was because he lived on a side Road and out of the Path of Civilization.

The Ioway Person, when found, did not seem in a Position or Mood to Hurry to pay. The Head Salesman thought he would see if he could infuse a little Enthusiasm into him on that Subject. He went and saw a Lawyer and gave him a Retainer—which the Lawyer, needless to say, Retained—and armed the Sheriff with enough Legal Documents to paper the Interior of the Auditorium. He had discovered that the Timber belonged to another Party and that the Iowa Person was sawing by Contract and keeping his Account with his Customer pretty well

RESAWED FABLES

overdrawn all the time. There were some other Things that he did not discover until later.

The Head Salesman said he would make one more Effort and told the Sheriff to come out there Saturday Morning and do his Duty. The Head Salesman went out himself Friday p.m. He Told the Iowa Person if he didn't produce before Nightfall he would attach the whole Works. He Sat up until 11:37 that Night waiting for the Dough that never came. Then he went to Bed and awaited the Coming of the Sheriff.

They drove out to the Place together. The Portable Saw Mill had been moved a hundred Feet during the Night. "Do Your Duty," said the Head Salesman. "Can't," said the Sheriff. "Why Not?" asked the Head Salesman. "This is the State Line there and that Saw Mill is now in Minnesota." Then the Head Salesman knew why the Ioway Person wanted a Portable Mill.

The Sheriff and the Head Salesman drove back to Town. "What are you going to do?" asked one of the Leading Citizens, who was leading a Mule at the Time. "Go over into Minnesota and start Proceedings over there." "Don't you do it," said the Leading Citizen, "Please Don't Do It; he might move back. You leave these Papers with our Sheriff and we'll make up a Purse and pay you for your Mill."

Moral—The World admires Energy; the Man who keeps Moving often finds People willing and anxious to help him along.

Of Talking Out in Meeting

In a City of about 202,718 Population, or possibly 202,719, there was a man who made Something of a Success of the Wholesale Lumber Business. In Consequence he had his Picture printed in a Book containing the Bitter Past of the Main People of Minnesota, and his Name had been mentioned in connection with Congress, although never when Congress was Around. His Beginning was comparatively Humble. When he started in his Equipment consisted of a Rolltop Desk, a Stenographer, who was willing to wait for her Money as long as she could tell her Friends she had a Job, and an Office up a back Stairway in a Building on a back Street that was called an Office Building because it was never heated in Winter. His Capital amounted to $857.39 and a Faculty for hypnotizing Mill Men into believing that he was one of the largest Operators in Minnesota. As he weighed around 239 there may have been some Truth in this. Most Lumbermen are too busy getting wealthy to take the Time to get fat.

Fortune smiled on this Man like a Soubrette and ere many Years he had built up a Wholesale Business and a row of Correspondence Files that were the Envy of every Man who dropped around his Way who was suffering with a Desire to butt into the Wholesale Lumber Trade. It could not be expected that the People who Got Next to his Prosperity were going to Let his Business get stale because of a Lack of Competition.

One Day a Gazaboo with a Suit of Soprano Clothes and a Shrill Necktie wandered into his Place and told him he wanted to write the Wholesaler up for a Book entitled: "How the Well-Bred People Made Their Dough." He acquired some Minute Details on the Method by which the Wholesaler had got his Start and how he had been able to keep up the Pace. These things he wrote down in a Red Morocco Note Book just like a regular Literary Man wouldn't.

In about a Fortnight the Guy with the Red Morocco Notebook and the Vociferous Necktie blossomed out with a Rival Wholesale Lumber Business that was going to sweep the Other Fellow off the Earth. He began cutting into the Other Fellow's Trade, or at least making a Noble Stab at it. About a Week Later he thought it would be a Good Idea to send an Emissary around to see how the Other Fellow was Taking it. There is always Somebody standing around willing to do a Job of this Kind, and that is what makes Good People lonesome. The Trusted Emissary happened around to the Other Fellow's Yard one Day. That is the Way he explained it.

"I just Happened around," said the Emissary to the Wholesale Man.

"A Man can never Tell," replied the Wholesale Man, "what is Going to Happen."

This reply staggered Humanity, at least that Part of it represented by the Trusted Emissary. However, he and the Wholesale Man were soon on quite Friendly Terms. Finally the Trusted Emissary hitched his Chair up to the Confidential distance of 2 feet and 3 inches and, lowering his Voice about the Same Distance, inquired:

"Now, between You and Me—it won't go any Further—what's your Opinion of this New Wholesaler and what are his Chances of Success?"

"I'll tell you," said the Wholesaler, "and you needn't make any Secret of it—You can go tell Him if you want to. I don't think his Chances are very Good. I know he's a crook and I know he's a Liar."

This Surprised the Trusted Emissary Somewhat by its Bluntness; but not so much as the Reply of the New Wholesale Man when it was conveyed to him.

"Well," quoth that Worthy Gentleman, "I guess I'll have to Bunch it. If he had Lied about me behind my Back I would have Stood some Show; but darn the Man who Talks Right out in Meeting."

Moral—Nothing is so Inexplicable to a Liar as the Truth.

Of Getting an Audience

A man who showed no other Symptoms of Insanity once became inoculated with the Idea that he would be a Big Hit on the Lecture Platform. He thought he could make Burton Holmes and Richmond Pearson Hobson and Jasper E. Brady look like a lot of Jayhawkers from the Tall and Uncut. He dreamed Visions of one night Stands and packed Houses and palatial Hotels and long stenographic Reports in the Newspapers, accompanied by Halftones. He believed he had it in him to move vast Concourses, to move the Young, the Old, the Sentimental, the Prosaic—in fact, to do a general Moving Business. He believed he could make

Demosthenes go 'way back, and cause Bill Bryan to go and get a Rep.

An equally irresponsible Lecture Bureau, whose Ideals were so high they occupied the Back Room of the Top Floor of a Minneapolis Skyscraper, booked the Lecturer for a Tour around the Country, agreeing to give him 40 percent of the Gross and taking 20 itself. Then the Orator went home and wrote a Few Lectures so as to have a Rip-or-tore. After February 1 he turned himself loose on the Startled World. In the Days of the Ancients, when the Banks of the Nile were Pharaoh Banks and the Panama Canal had just been started, there were Soothsayers who used to make as much as $13.75 a week interpreting Dreams. They could take a Hungarian Goulash or Welsh Rarebit Dream and interpret it into fairly readable English. In this modern Day the Great Dream interpreter is Experience.

The Lecturer had not been long En Tour before cold, hard Experience began to interpret his Dreams of packed Houses, palatial Hotels etc. He found an Audience was as hard to get at Oshkosh as at the Court of St. James. The Spectators used to take Pity on him and come down and sit in one Row so as to keep him Company. For two Weeks he had a Lonesome Time, never seeing a Human Face. He saw nothing but

Hotel Clerks and Stage Hands. The Hotels were palatial all right; but the Palace they resembled was the old Montreal Ice Palace. Only one newspaper had the Nerve to print his Cut and that was what Shakespeare called "the most unkindest Cut of All." Shakespeare may have been grammatically Bum when he penned that Line but his prophetic Soul sized up the American Cartoonist Centuries before John McCutcheon was born. Thanks to a Combination of Cheap Print and summer Ink, this Cut of the Lecturer indicated he had just broken out with the Measles or from Jail

Fortunately for the Lecturer, he had a Friend in the Retail Lumber Business up in the Twin Cities and he sent him enough Money to get Home to the Wheat State. These two Men had a Way of talking to each Other as plain as Print in a Primer.

"I've been watching your Mad Career," said the Lumberman, after they had gripped, "and I'll tell you what was the Matter with your Lectures. It wasn't because you weren't eloquent, for you were; it wasn't because your Shirt Front wouldn't keep Inside your low-necked Vest, for it did. The Trouble was this: You lectured to the Wrong People. When you spoke at the Banquet of the Captains of Industry it was on 'Living on Ten Dollars a Week.' To the

Ladies' Bridge Club you Talked on 'The Art of Bread Making.' You never had an Audience that was likely to be Interested in what you talked About."

The Lecturer had Picked up a Paper.

"How's Business?" he asked.

"None too good," replied the Lumberman.

"Why don't you Advertise?"

"I do; but it doesn't seem to do any Good."

"Want to Know Why?"

"Don't I spend Enough?"

"Too much; but you don't reach the Right People. Here's your Ad in a Paper that Don't Reach Anybody but Women looking for Millinery Bargains. Why don't you Advertise in some Paper that hits the Folks who Build Houses? Seems to Me that other People have been Talking to the Wrong Audience."

This fable has both a Moral and a Sequel. The Sequel is that the Lumber Dealer is doing one of the nicest Businesses done in Minnesota and the Lecturer is making Money as his and other Men's Advertising Specialist. The following is the

Moral—Advertising is like a Seance; you can't materialize the Right Spirit with the Wrong Medium.

Of Taking a Few Days Off

Once upon a Time there was a Mill Man who was so busy that he used to Yearn for a Leap Year so that he could get in an extra Day's Work. He was as busy as a Man from Strawberry Point, Iowa, dodging street Cars and Gold Brick Retailers on State street or a Coal Baron making Excuses at the Pearly Gates. Old Rand McNally, whom we read about in Mythology as being the Chap who carried the World around on his Shoulders, had a Cinch when considered beside this Busy Individual, who toted around a Saw Mill and a few Office Fixtures, a hundred thousand acres of pine Land and a Bad Digestion. This Mill Man was so busy that when he ate he shoveled his Grub in like a Man feeding Cedar Sawdust to a Furnace. His Wife had to use Force to get him to eat Breakfast and at Noon he lunched on Mince Pie and Buttermilk, washed down with Coffee as strong as a Ragtime Singer at a Stag Party. He dined on Roast Beef served with Walnut Quotations and Turnip Salad, garnished with the Poplar Outlook.

When Christmas Day came bumping along this Busy Man had at least to run down and open his Mail, and it took him so Long he had to eat a Christmas Dinner made up of Cold Turkey and wobbly Cranberry Jelly. It was the Same at New Year's. When Washington's Birthday fell on Sunday the Industrious Individual laughed a Fiendish Laugh because that meant no Loss of Time. Most People took Monday off to make up for it, but not the Busy Boy. This fateful Monday he made his usual Suicidal Lunch and that Night he dreamed a Dream. Do you Wonder?

He Meandered through Dreamland and he met a Jolly Little Man.

"Who are You?" he asked of the Humorous Little Personage.

"I am Death."

"But I thought Death a Skeleton."

"Once I was, but Busy People have made me Fat."

"What are You doing with the Book and Pen?"

"I am taking a Few Days Off."

"No, you are working."

"Oh, they're not my Days I am taking Off. They're yours."

"How's that?"

"Did you take a Day Off Christmas Day?"

"No."

"New Year's?"

"N-no."

"I did."

"What do you Mean?"

"Every time you have failed to take a Day off during your Life I have taken a Few Off the End of your Life."

"Then I'm nothing ahead?"

"Nothing, according to my Bookkeeping—and I'm a Pretty Fair Bookkeeper."

Then the Busy Man woke up.

Moral—No man can rob Himself and not be a Loser.

Of the Point of View

There lingered in Montana some Years back a Saw Mill Man who had a Backbone like a Piece of Spring Steel. Whenever he Took a Position he held on to it like a Politician fastens his Hooks into a Job. Once he got an Idea wedged into his Brain, it was as hard to get Out as the Republican Vote on a Rainy Day. Every Idea grows more or less after it gets a start; but an Idea in this Man's Think Tank took such Root that it couldn't have been combed out with a Stump Puller.

This Man had put $21,000 and Ten of the best Years of his Life into this Saw Mill, and this had given him the crazy Idea he Owned it. Foolish

Man. When some well-meaning Individual happened around and offered to Show this Montana Saw Mill Man how to run his Mill the Saw Mill Man told him to Run Along.

He was about the Poorest market for advice in the State. Anybody who tried to Hypnotize him would have to Pull Chloroform and a Club on him to do it. Every time he told an Advisory Committee to go chase Itself the Town called it another Sample of the Saw Mill Man's Obstinacy and Stubbornness.

One day, nevertheless, they elected this man Mayor of the Town. This entitled him to 300 Simoleons a Year and a Pass to the Local Theater. It is pretty hard for a Man to run a Saw Mill and a Town at the same Time. (The Lumbermen who have tried it will Please not "Amen" so Loudly.) One mellow Spring an Electric Railway Company got the Impression it was going to lay a Track and String a few Dozen Wires down the Street without giving any Assurances that it would Observe the Rights of the Common People. When it couldn't get the Council's Permission it got Gay and began laying Rails with the Enthusiasm and Cheerfulness of a Bridegroom putting down his first Carpet. The Mayor tried an Injunction first and, when that didn't work, he took an Ax. The local Paper wrote several long Columns about his

"Fixedness of Purpose" and "Unyielding Determination" and People slapped him on the Back.

Moral—Human Virtues, as Judged by Human Minds, are largely a Question of the Point of View.

Of Letting Loose

This is the Time of Year when a Man with a thousand Dollar Salary turns himself Loose and spends Coin like a Millionaire trying to Make Good at the Press Club. The Christmas Feeling is in the Air and the Boulevards of every Burg from New York, N. Y., to Shillabah, Ore., are congested with People out Buying for Other People Things that the other People don't Want. It is a Game without a Limit or a Thought of Consequences. A Thrifty young Man may start out with a Twenty in his Clothes, intending to buy his Best Girl a seventy-five Cent Purse, and come Home owing the Jeweler Money.

For Some People this is a Good Thing, for, if it were not for the Merry Christmas Season, their Poor Relations would never know they were Living. Then is the Time they Loosen; and in Consequence the Nephew in Central Lake, Mich., or the Maiden Aunt in Harveyville, Kan., gets Some Ormolu Truck, and the Other Members of the Family are likewise Remembered. Many a Man would Pass in his Checks from Contraction of the Heart were it not that he Passed Out his Checks to his Poor Relations at Christmas. As the Lifer Remarked when he shinned down a Bedquilt, it's a Good Thing for People to let themselves Out once in a while.

Once upon a Time there was one Crusty old Bachelor Tallyman—only One. Bachelors in Stories are always Old and always Crusty— Crusty, perhaps, because they Partake of so much indigestible Boarding House Pie. Any Man who has ever dragged in his Trunk and dragged out his Existence in a Boarding House knows that there is Nothing so Durable as Pie. Often a gray haired Old Boarder will be handed a Piece of Pie that is just like Mother used to make—so much so, in Fact, that he is Inclined to believe it is some she did make, though the Good Soul has been gone these Forty Years.

Living on a Diet composed largely of this Three-Ply Pie Crust, the Old Bachelor approached Christmas with no Thrill of Joy. He saw the Advertisements in the Newspapers, the Decorations in the Windows, the Increased Attendance in the Sunday Schools, and Other Infallible Signs of the Christmas Season, but he said he wasn't going to buy Anything for Anybody because he Knew nobody was going to buy Anything for him. Let 'em have their Christmas and he'd have his. They were a Pack of Fools anyhow for Blowing in their Money for a Lot of Trash that would do Good to Nobody but the Man who sold it at 90 percent Profit. The Shysters wouldn't get any of his Money.

It was soliloquizing somewhat in this Fashion that he Set out a few evenings before Christmas to buy himself a Cigar. The Snow was blowing around like a second Rate Prize Fighter and the Steam was freezing on the Hateful Windows with their Displays of Christmas Trash. Beating his Way against the Wind and Turning and Tacking like a man laying a Stair Carpet, in Front of a Toy Shop he fell over the Small Figure of a Boy crouched on the Sidewalk. He stumbled into a recently formed Snow Drift and the Fall did not much Improve his Temper.

He arose and Brushed the Snow from his Clothes. Then he seized the Youngster by the Arm and inquired:

"What do you Mean by Getting in People's Way? Come, out with it!"

"You see, Mister," said the boy, beginning to Weep, "there's a fine Soldier in the Window there and ev'ry Night I come up here and bid him Goodbye. I'm Allus afraid Someone may have bought him and carried him Away. Well,

Tonight the Window was all Frosty an' I thought if I held my Cheek against it maybe the Frost would Melt so I could see if he was There. An' then you Fell over me. So I don't know whether he's There or not, but I guess he is, 'cause I guess there ain't nobody Likely to Buy him. You see my Sister told me that the Store man wanted a Dollar for him. I'll go home now, but I wish I could say Goodnight to the Soldier before I go. But the Window's too frosty.''

Then a Remarkable Thing happened to the Crusty Old Bachelor Tallyman. He dragged the Frightened Boy into that Toy Store. What if the Gay Soldier had been Sold? The more he thought about it the More he hurried, pulling the Boy off his Feet. A Clerk came up and asked him if he was being Waited on, when he Knew Perfectly well he Wasn't. The Tallyman didn't know how to ask for what he Wanted. Then an Idea struck him and he held the Boy up so he could Look into the Window.

"There he is," cried the Boy in Glee. "Nobody ain't Bought him. Goodnight, Soldier. Now, Mister, I'll go Home.''

A Minute Later the Crusty Old Bachelor found himself throwing his Money away on a Lot of Christmas Trash. First of all was the Soldier and then some Dolls for the two Little

Sisters the Boy said he had, and Candy for the Whole Family.

It was some Time before the Crusty Old Tallyman reached the Cigar Store, but when he did he bought himself a Box. He hadn't Felt so Well in Ten Years.

Moral—A Man ought to be Thankful for Little Children if for no Other Reason than that it is so Easy to make them Happy.

Of Swinging Back

Fame is one of the queerest Things in the World. Men have shot the Whirlpool Rapids or their Neighbors in Hopes of acquiring it, but Fame has Given them only the Icy Stare; but Small Boys have waved Red Flannel Shirts in Front of Trains going to their Doom, or Abilene, Kan., or some other Place, and acquired Fame without Effort or Premeditation. From all of which it must not necessarily be Drawn that a Red Flannel Shirt is better than Endeavor in getting Famous, any more than a Four Flush is better than an Ace Full just because it gives Excuse for a successful Bluff a little Less Often than Once in a While.

There is a Lumber Dealer in St. Louis who

has acquired Fame among his Brethren all at Once, although he did not go into the Highways and Byways and look for it or walk about with a Lightning Rod concealed along his Spinal Column, hoping it would strike him. That kind of Effort never seems to pay any Dividends. The Writer has been going around with his Lightning Rod up for, oh, these Many Years, but when he buys a Meal Ticket at the Bismarck the Girl still asks him how he Spells his name. Fame is about as Skittish as a Three-Year-Old, and about as apt to run away after you think you have it safely Broken to Harness.

This St. Louis wholesaler is not One of the 5,799 St. Louisians who first conceived the Idea of a Louisiana Purchase Exposition. Neither did he ever wave any Red Flannel Shirts in Front of any Cattle Trains. Fame came to him like a Summer Sigh. He did not go out looking for Fame; instead, when he went forth Fame appeared to be looking for him, like a Loose Sign over a Doorway that never lets go until it can Soak on the Head someone who is Passing Out.

A few Days after New Year's there was a Sound in St. Louis like the Popping of ten million Firecrackers. The noise was produced by People all over St. Louis who were Breaking Resolutions. It was a gay yet mournful Sound to hear Resolutions that in December looked so Strong and Healthy, breaking down like an Aunt at a Wedding, the first week in January. It was in such a Night, as Shakespeare would have said if he had written this, that the Lumberman went forth.

It was the Hotel Clerk who said it.

"Have you seen 'em?" he asked.

"Who?" asked the Lumberman, meaning whom.

"The Bunch," answered the Man with the Pen on his ear and Inkspots on his Manly Bosom.

Now the Bunch were all known to the Lumberman.

"Why?" he asked.

"You deserve a Medal," said the Clerk. "You're the only One of the Gang that isn't out Breaking his New Year's Resolutions."

"So?" said the Man of Boards.

The Clerk looked at him Admiringly.

"Tell me," he asked, "How did you Manage to do it?"

"Hist," replied the Lumberman, leaning over the Desk, "I'll put you Next: I never made Any."

Moral—Many a New Year's Resolution is only a Pendulum in Disguise.

Of the Gentle Game of Golf

When Handel Bords was a Wee Urchin who had Urched only Seven Summers, his Governor, that is his Old Man, that is his Dad, that is his Father, called him into his Private Office in the Blacksmith Shop and imparted to him a few Wads of Wisdom.

"Handel," chirped the Old Man, "You are named for a Great Man and I don't want to see you Go Wrong. This Gazabo for whom your Mother named you was the lightweight Champion of the Ivory Keys. There was never but one man in the Business in later years who Could Put it Over Him, and that was Wagner, the Heavyweight. Wagner had more Steam, but he wasn't a bit shiftier than Han was when he hooked up for Twenty Rounds with the Pianoforte."

"Yes, papa."

"Being named after two great men like Handel and Me, it is up to you to follow the brilliant Example we have made for you. Your Old Dad may be Called Away at Any Time. No, my son, not by the Sheriff. Before I go, I would impart some Counsel.

"This it is—never play Another Man's Game. Did Wellington accept Napoleon's offer to Roll the Bones at Waterloo? No, sir—and he got Boots named after him. Did Cæsar ever Settle a Battle with Ping-Pong? No, sir—and Shakespeare Wrote a Play about him. If you would learn a new game, learn it from the Editor of the Village Weekly, so the money will go for a Good Cause."

As the boy grew to the Age of Wisdom and a Fuzzy Chin he remembered his Father's words —long, long after the Sheriff arrived. He sidestepped Poker, he Only Flirted with Bridge, and he told people that Pit was Wicked. He never Indicated the Elusive Pea under the Shell, nor did he become a depositor in a Faro Bank. As a result, Handel was Variously Accounted a Perfectly Lovely Man or a Dead One, according to the Point of View.

But one day along about June 27 a. m. one Bob Knox aforethought invited Handel Bords to make the Morning Round at the Golf Tournament, in order to get limbered up for the Afternoon Play. Handel told Bob he wasn't Taking a Thing. Then Bob explained that he wanted him to Play Golf, Golf, don't you understand?— Golf!

Handel Bords, not wishing to show his Ignorance, which Inventoried Large, accepted the Invitation and a Bunch of Walking Canes with deadly looking hammers on the ends. Not knowing that it was Necessary to have a Boy to do the Heavy Work, he Hoisted it Himself.

Then Bob placed a small white Globule on top of a Mud Pile and told Handel to Soak it. No, gentle reader, Handel did not Miss it. He Soaked it 165 yards, made the first hole in bogey, and beat Bob 5 up and 4 to play.

Moral—The youngster who Believes all the Old Man says Misses a lot of the Good Things of Life. The Game that Beat the Old Man may be the Young Man's Meat.

Of Silence That Isn't So Golden

The Man was Locoed on the Subject of Doing Business in a Business Way. He believed in System. He talked System in his sleep. Life to him was one grand Card Index. The reason was, perhaps, that he had a nervous System himself that was geared up to 60 Miles per hr. By close attention to Righteous Precepts and Vertical Filing Cabinets he had built up a Large and Lucrative Lumber Practice. He ran a local Retail Lumber Emporium and did a considerable business in Piece Stuff and Such. He made some of the Rhino in this Wise; and he attributed his Success to the Business way in which his Business was run. It might also be mentioned that he attributed the Business Way to himself.

This man had certain rules which he had had printed on White Wedding Bristol with a Red Border. These were pasted in Conspicuous Places about the office. A free Translation of a few of these Epigrammatic Efforts will be about as follows, to-wit:

> NEVER SPEAK UNTIL SPOKEN TO—AND SOMETIMES NOT THEN.
>
> A SOFT ANSWER TURNETH AWAY WRATH, IF NOT TOO SOFT; BUT IT ALSO TAKETH TIME.
>
> HONOR THY FATHER AND THY MOTHER—BUT NOT A STRANGER'S CHECKS.
>
> TO ERR IS HUMAN; BLESSED ARE THE INHUMAN.
>
> YOU CAN WIN BY PERSEVERANCE; BUT YOU MAY LOSE BY STUBBORNNESS.

The Systematic man allowed these were Pretty Nifty; he thought also that they ought to be, seeing that he had written them Himself, with the Accent on the Himself. He was particularly struck with that top one, which he had suspended over the Office Boy's cell.

Office Boys, as a Rule, are too Stingy with

Silence. They are always chewing gum or language. Of course you will Immediately show these lines to your office Boy, so a few remarks will be injected for his Benefit. Unfortunately when they tell Things about you outside the Office they tell the Truth. The head Bookkeeper jollies you along with something Different. The head Bookkeeper is looking for Advancement. The office boy isn't looking for Advancement— he Expects it.

This boy read the Handwriting on the Wall and was Wise. It said, "Never Speak until Spoken to—and Sometimes Not then." There had been other Boys before him. They held neither their Tongues nor their Jobs. This boy was Pointed out by the Man as a Model, just as the Sign was a Model Sign.

One day the Systematic Man heard a 4-11, or thought he did.

"Willie," he said, "Go out and see if there ain't a Fire."

Willie went out as per Instructions. In a few Minutes he returned and began worrying the Office Cat some more. Once he started suddenly; then his eyes fell on the Sign, and he remembered his Job.

Five minutes later the Systematic Man inquired:

"Well, is there a Fire?"

"Yes, sir," replied the boy, as succinctly as Possible.

Ten minutes passed. Then the Boss turned in his Swivel chair again.

"What is it?" he asked of the Office Boy, casually.

"Your East Yard."

Moral—Plain Common Sense is a Safer Bet than a Hand-Painted Motto.

Of What Rip Saw

He owned Eighty Acres of Blonde Sand up in Roscommon county and he Thought that this Forest Reserve Foolishness was Trespassing on the Rights of Free-Born Citizens. When the Forestry Commission ran Fire Lines and did a few other Nonsensical Things on the Eighty next to him and the 160 acres across the Road, he thought that the Free-Born Citizens aforesaid should Rise Up in arms and Chase the Rude Invaders back to the State Capitol. His neighbors thought Likewise, but somehow they didn't Rise. There must have been something the matter with the Yeast.

This man's Eighty had Once been covered with Oak, but it had been Cleaned off by the Lumber-

men. The Oak, however, did not act Mean about
It. After the Lumbermen had Cut it down Close
and left it looking like a Shingled Poodle, the
Life of the Oak was still There; and it Sprang
up Anew like the Phoenix bird or the Alderman
from the Sixth.

However, the Free-Born Citizen saw to that.
He had only about Thirty acres under Cultiva-
tion, but he ran Fire through the Other Fifty
and Turned Sheep and Sunday school Picnics
and other Destructive Forces Loose in it to keep
the Oak from getting too firm a Hold. He said
he didn't want to have to Clear that Eighty
Twice.

One day this man fell into a Trance. There
had been a Suspicion ever since he began Buck-
ing the Forestry Commission that he was Walking in his Sleep. The Neighbors who discovered
him in a Trance sent for a Doctor, who gave him
stuff to make him Wake up, but he only Turned
over on the other Side and Snored in an exas-
perating Basso Profundo manner.

This Rip Van Winkle II had the original Rip
beaten a block. The Detroit newspaper boys got
wind of it and they worked the Sleeping Beauty
of Roscommon county for all he was worth. The
Probate Court of Roscommon also Worked Overtime. Someone had to look after Rip II's affairs.
When the Doctor couldn't do anything, the

Neighbors sent for the Coroner, but he Said he Couldn't Do Anything, either. They wanted him to hold an Inquest, but he declined to hold an Inquest on a Man who was Still Alive. They had found $133.17 in the Man's Bunk and it was Finally decided to turn this over to the Probate Court after the Sheriff had refused to Interfere. The Sheriff said he Wasn't going to make himself Liable by Arresting the man. He said it was no Crime to Fall Asleep.

The Probate Judge was up a Stump. It isn't hard to get up a Stump in Roscommon county, for there are plenty of them. He couldn't enter the case as "Deceased" or "Insane" or anything like that. Finally he entered the man as "Asleep" and appointed a Guardian for him. The Guardian kept the Taxes paid up and went around every 22nd of September to see if the Man had come to.

Meanwhile the Forestry Commission was Busily at work. The Commission was not asleep, if its neighbor was. It encouraged Reseeding on its land, watched for Fires, and gave Mother Nature all the Encouragement that was Proper.

One day, after the Expiration of the Customary One Hundred years, the Rip Van Winkle of Roscommon county dreamed that England had Lifted the Cup. Then he Woke up.

The Oak Timber on his Fifty uncultivated Acres brought him $33,711.99 at the Mill.

Moral — If you want to know how Mother Nature stands on the Question of Reforestation, just leave her alone a Few Years.

Of Bow Ling Ali and the Man with the Stump Puller

Bow Ling Ali was Shaykh of the village of Hi Bal, an Oasis in the desert half way between Dri Nek and Par Esis. Over such of his Dependents as had not already sailed for Pittsburg to sell Plaster of Paris Images he ruled with a firm, almost a corporation, hand. These inhabitants of the Skin-tent village were wont to call him the All-Wise. In the evenings they would Coagulate near his tent door and sing a Serenade:

> All-Wise, All-Wise, we will love you always;
>   Do not fear—our love is true,
>   For we live alone on you.
> All-Wise, All-Wise, we will love you always;
>   Love like ours is always true
> And it lives always, All-Wise.

This song (B. C. 617) is still sung in America, in an Aggravated form.

Being the only Visible means of Support that numerous of the villagers possessed, Shaykh Bow Ling Ali was considerable of a Poo-Bah; for the people responded by Handing him all the Public Offices to which no Salary was attached. One of these Jobs was that of Chief Magistrate. As there was no appeal from his Decisions, he exercised all the power of an absolute monarch. If he called a man Safe at Second the man was safe, even if he was seven feet off the Bag. The very Finality of his judgment gave him a Rep for being a wise Gazabo.

One day there blew into the Village a man from Chicago who was selling Stump Pullers. He said this Stump Puller would raise anything in the tented village—and he gave a Demonstration by pulling up a number of Date Palms. These Date Palms were large Palms under which the village maidens of three Generations had kept their Dates.

Now when the American in Ten Minutes lifted out a date palm that had been a Hundred Years in getting a Good Hold the villagers began to feel that a Wise One had come along and that he would make Bow Ling Ali look like a plate of Ice Cream in the Business part of a Blast Furnace.

This rumor came to Bow Ling Ali and he caused the man from Chicago to be brought before him. The Shaykh received him, seated on a magnificent Oriental Rug for which he had paid $19.98 at a Fire Sale.

"Milk-strained skinner, or rather milk-skinned stranger," the Shaykh began, "thou hast a machine which will lift Anything?"

"That I have, coffee-colored Caliph."

"We shall See."

Whereupon the Shaykh caused a great iron-bound stake to be brought and twenty men were employed for Half an Hour to drive it into the Earth. But the Yankee with the Business for Pulling the Teeth out of the Face of Nature yanked the Stake out in a minute and sixteen seconds.

At this the populace wondered; and it looked like the Yankee had Made a few Votes.

"There is one more Test," said Bow Ling Ali, the All-Wise, "and if you fail in this you may have your Choice of being Boiled in Oil or being Elocuted by one of our female Elocutionists; either, I think, thou wilt find sufficiently Horrible. If your iron demon will lift Anything, cause it to lift the Mortgage off the Royal Tomb."

This was where the man from Chicago got off and panted for breath. But they slung him into a Dark and Dismal Dungeon and sent for the Elocutionist. Twenty minutes after the

Arrival of the Elocutionist the Shaykh sent word to the machinery salesman that if his Machine could Raise $200 all would be forgiven and he could Move On.

The stranger had $127.23 and they Compromised. In the Village of Hi Bal Confidence was Restored.

Moral—Many a man thinks he has a Pull that is a Cinch—until he Really has to Pull Something.

Of Seeing the World

Dame Fortune and the Chicago & North-Western railway once brought two Families into a small Jerkwater Town at about the same Time. The Town was so small that a Man going Home from Lodge had to step carefully in order to keep within the Village Limits. The Town was so small, in fact, that, although the name of one Family was Smith and that of the other Jones, they were the only Joneses and Smiths in the Village.

The Smith family had a Cow, a Clothes Wringer, the Grandfather of a Horse and one Son. That was all the Furniture it Possessed.

The Jones Family was better off. It had not only a Son, but it had also a Picture

Album and Money in a St. Paul bank. It had moved around Minnesota and Wisconsin considerably, because it was cheaper than paying Grocery Bills.

The Smith Family had, up to this time, lived on a Sand Farm for Generations and had moved to preserve the Family Name, which was in danger of Extermination because of poor crops. Smith, Sr., felt that he had done his Full Duty by the Old Homestead, and Felt no Compunction when he yielded to a Desire for some other kind of a Meal besides Oatmeal and Cornmeal.

Young Smith and Young Jones went to School together. They fought, bit and lied for one Another. But though their Sympathies and Kite Strings were in Common, they differed in their Ambitions. Young Jones determined to see Something of the World. He started out at 15 in Deadly Earnest and a Box Car, but came back when a Brakeman sneaked up behind him and Suggested it to him. When he started again he was 18, and this time went for Sure. He began work in a Saw Mill at Ashland, and then drifted to Appleton. He spent a Winter in the U. P., and got down to Chicago one Summer. At Ashland he had learned how to make Lumber; in the U.P. he had learned how to get Logs out; and in Chicago he Learned something about the Selling Part. He worked as far West as

Salt Lake, as far South as Memphis, and as far East as Pittston, though he was careful not to work Too Much. After a few Years of this he concluded he had satisfied his Boyish Ambition to see the World. He did not know that there was still Some of the World left east of Pittston and south of Memphis. However, he decided to go back to the Old Town on the C. & N.-W. and exhibit his Three-Ounce Watch-charm.

Meanwhile the Smith Boy did not Exhibit any such Ambition or Brocaded Vest. He stuck right to the Old Burg and showed no disposition to get into a Bigger Place. Many a Man has started his Career in a County Jail and by Diligence and Study and Application to Business has climbed up and up until he has occupied a Place in some of the Leading Penitentiaries of the Country. Not so the Smith boy. He Stuck to Mother and Father. The Result was that when the Jones boy came back he found the Smith Boy holding down a Chair in front of the Village Store. The Town had grown some by the Padding of some new Additions, and So had the Smith boy. Otherwise Things were unchanged.

"Well," said the Jones fellow, "I'm glad I got out of this Hole. I'm Getting $125 per with a Chicago wholesale Lumber House now. Still stick to the Old Town, don't you, Smith?"

"Yes," replied Smith; "I have to."
"No, you don't Have to—there's a Chance for any Chap out in the Great World."
"I know, but I kind of Feel that I'd ought to Stick to the Old Town."
"Nonsense! Why?"
"I own most of it."
Moral—A Meandering Stone accumulates no Lichen.

Of Helping Others

"The surest way to help Yourself," quoth the Youth in his Graduation essay, "is to help someone Else. I do not mean to help yourself to what someone else Has."

Then he paused, that his Words might sink Deep into the souls of his auditors—and also because the professor of public speaking had told him that was a good place to Catch his Breath.

"What I mean," said the Graduate, "is to help someone else First and then help yourself."

Father, who had worn a glad White Tie all day at the mill in honor of the august occasion, was sitting well down in Front.

"In other words," thought father to himself, "let some in on the ground floor—that is helping

Others; but when it becomes time to declare a Dividend, help yourself."

The Graduate, however, did not know that his father had misinterpreted his Logic — or rather his graduation essay. The Graduate thought the essay was pretty good. He was frank enough to admit that to Mother, who thought it was Just Splendid.

The youth was at least conscientious and consistent. After he had left School and started out in the wide, wide, and moderately thick World, he tried to put his altruistic principles into active Practice. He went to Chicago—in a Pullman car—to study the social settlements. He Slummed it—and it cost father about $73.48 per Slum.

He knew he was doing a good deal of Good, because the Pastor of the Highland Park church Told him so. One day he was out slumming in an Automobile and accidentally ran across an old Friend. He told the old friend about the good Work he was doing and how he expected to have his home for broken-down Hash Slingers open by the first of August.

"I hope you do," said the old friend, frankly, "because I don't think the Old Man will Hold Out much longer than that."

The Graduate wondered what He meant. He went Home to find out. He found that Father was running a big Saw Mill and running it alone. Father told him that there wasn't anybody around just then that he liked to trust many of the Things to except him, and he was busy with his Great Work. Father looked about as Robust, when he said it, as a man in a 6-day bicycle Race at the end of the 13,721st lap.

The Graduate decided that the home of the broken-down hash slingers could wait.

Moral—Help yourself by helping Others—but help your own Others before you help other people's others.

Of the Light That Failed

Once there were two Unfortunates who had Both been caught by Dame Fortune with Lumber Yards on them and Treated accordingly. When that Lady captures a Yap with such Evidences of Reckless Disregard of Consequences on his Person, what she Does to him is Good and Plenty and Some More. She does not like Anything better than to find a Retail Yard man somewhere and Impale him on an Injunction or an Execution and then Broil him over a Slow Lawsuit. The Mills of the Law-Gods grind Slowly, but they Pulverize middling fine. When they get Hold of an Innocent and Unsophisticated lumberman they Reduce him to Blue Vapor.

When Dame Fortune found these two yard men with the Goods on them she unbottled a Building Boom. Now, that would Ordinarily seem to be very Lovely of her. A Building Boom ought to be Meat to a Lumber dealer. But a Building Boom is sometimes a Boomerang. It gives a Yard man Fancy Ideas. He begins to Load Up. He gets the Crazy Notion that his Burg is going to show an increase in Population. He may have a Few Measly Millions Piled in his Yards, but he gets the Impression that he can treble his Profits by doubling his Stock. Of course, all he trebles is his Insurance, his Taxes, his Bills Payable and his Troubles. There is no Reason why a Yard man should Treble his Troubles. There is no Crying necessity for it. If he Wants Trouble a Simpler method is to Marry.

These two Yard men were Hit by this Building Boom, and they Started to clean up Wholesale stocks in the East. They wanted to get a Corner in Lumber. Now, any Man who sets out to get a Corner in Lumber generally never gets anything Better than a Nice quiet Corner in a Cemetery. If a Retailer wishes to Land out in Forest Lawn he Should get the radical Idea that he is not carrying enough Lumber for the Prospective

Demand. The prospective demand is not infrequently an Ignis Fatuus that will Lead him into Muck that is up to his Neck. Enough is enough.

These two Yard men began to Stock up. They bought Bevel Siding and Dimension, and Borrowed money and Trouble. Then a Railroad tore up its Tracks and put a Large Musical Puncture in the Building Boom through which the Escaping Gas whistled like a Messenger Boy.

One of these mis-dealers gritted his Teeth and Buckled in. He handed the Large juicy Jolly to his Creditors, and stood Collectors off with a gun. He lay awake at night and figured how to meet Notes the Next Day, and how Not to meet the Grocer. He moved a little Lumber at 5 off what he Paid for it, and in this Profitable manner managed to Keep his Standing in Church. He has just got now where he can Take a Long Breath without Feeling the pangs of Financial Pleurisy.

The other Dealer made no Attempt to Stem the Tide, and was declared a Bankrupt. He skipped all the Brain Fag and Moved to the Next Town, where his Address is now No. 1000 Easy Street.

Moral—Nothing Succeeds like a Failure.

Of the Sense of Touch

A Northern Mill Man was seated in his Palatial Office with his Pedal Extremities on a Desk constructed of Minnesota Mahogany and his back up against a magnificent Sofa Pillow which one of the Mill Hands of Artistic Tendencies had Constructed by Stuffing a Burlap Sack with Excelsior. He was Smoking a Missouri Meerschaum filled with Wisconsin Burley, and was as happy as a Landlord when a New Family moves in or an Old Family moves out. The Puffing of his Pipe kept time with the Puffing of an asthmatic Saw Mill outside. It was a warm Day in Summer, one of those days that fill the Air with the Incense of the Fields and Woods and make a Man feel Groggy. All Nature seemed at Rest, and most of the Lumber Shovers.

Down at the Water's Edge a Cricket sang its Song of Joy, but gave it up when a Boom Hand began to whistle "Hiawatha." The Pond Lilies floated idly on the Surface of the Boom, and the little Malaria Germs played Tag with the Typhoid Germs Next Door. As stated before, all Nature seemed at Rest. As a Poet would say, Nothing seemed to be sweating Itself.

Suddenly the Quiet of this Beautiful Pastoral Scene was busted by a Creature who projected his Form through the Office Door and Distributed himself over the Office Furniture. He was Tall and Thin, like a Piece of Asparagus, and as Seedy as a Sunflower. But he was Full of a Great Scheme, so Full of it that one could catch the Aroma of it on his Breath. These Tall and Seedy Strangers always are.

He introduced himself to the Mill Man before the Mill Man had Time to ask for an Introduction, and said he had just come in on the B. & O. —by which was probably Meant the Brakes and Oil-boxes. He had been looking timber down in Arkansas and he told the Mill Man he would put him Next to a scheme by which he could make a Million in Arkansaw Hemlock. The Mill Man had never heard much about Arkansas as a Hemlock producing State, but he permitted the Stranger to unfold his scheme.

The Long Continued Stranger said he didn't have much Ready Capital himself, but he was willing to let some Man who had in on the Great Scheme, with no Expectation of Reward. He said that in a Location in Arkansaw which he would mention later he had struck a Tract of 700,000 acres that he thought would run about 95 percent pure Hemlock to the Ton. The Outcroppings were very plain and he was only surprised that some other Prospector had not located the Timber long ago. He didn't have the Capital to work the Hemlock Claim himself, but he had secured an Option on 699,500 acres of it at $2.17 an acre, and if the Mill Man wanted to make a Million he would divulge the Locality.

"After you get Down there," said the Stranger, "and you find Everything as Represented, if you feel that you owe me a Little Something for putting you Next, why, it will be thankfully Received, as it will permit me to pursue my Art Studies in Europe. Some of the Old Masters are Anxious for me to Come over. A Little Commission wouldn't be any more than Fair, would it?"

"If I make a Million on the Deal," said the Mill Man, "I ought to give you $100,000, anyway."

"That's very kind of you," said the Stranger. "And, say, couldn't you let me have a Dollar and a Quarter of it now?"

This somewhat dampened the Mill Man's enthusiasm.

"I have always heard," he said, "that Riches were a Great Bother, so I guess I won't Monkey with your Generous Offer. In fact, I believe you are a Fakir, that you never was in Arkansas and you don't know any more about Looking Timber than a Hog does about the Hereafter."

At first the Stranger was inclined to protest;

but when he looked into the chilled steel Eyes of the Mill Man he admitted that the Jig was up.

"Tell me one thing," requested the Stranger as he collected himself together and prepared to Depart, "how did you find me out? Are you a Mind Reader?"

"No," replied the Mill Man; "I divine these things by the Sense of Touch."

Moral—Beware of the Stranger who would do you a Great Kindness but wants your Thanks in Advance.

Of the Savate Expert and the Man With the Spiked Boots

Being on the Main Line to Mecca, Shaykh Bow Ling Ali, Chief of the village of Hi Bal and owner of 700 horses and 21,000 camels, entertains many a Hadji on the Pilgrimage. He also entertains Others. One of these was M. Broyle, from Montreal, late of Paris, Savate expert in the Cafe de Bum Bum, just off the Rue M'Tism. M. Broyle could box with his head, hands and feet, and could lean his Face against an Opponent's Fist in a manner that was Marvelously Skillful.

It was his Foot Work, however, that threatened to make Famous the Cafe de Bum Bum. M. Broyle had tiny feet; but when he made a Feint with his Right Hand, an upper-cut with his Coco and a left swing with his Off Hoof, his opponent was led to believe that instead of scrapping with One Man he was surrounded by a Mob.

M. Broyle had not been long in the camp of Bow Ling Ali, the All-Wise, before the Wheelman of one of the ships of the desert discovered him Making Goo-Goo eyes at an Arabian Lady with a laundered flour-sack tied across her Eyes.

Thereupon there was a Wordy Altercation between the pilot of the dromedary and the Don Juan of the Cafe de Bum Bum. News of the Uproar came to the ear—in fact, both ears—of Bow Ling Ali, the All-Wise, and he had the Altercators brought before him. The courtroom of the Chief Magistrate of the Tribe was quickly filled, for the wisdom of Bow Ling Ali was great.

The Shaykh told each of the Contenders to state his case. "Well, monsieur," said M. Broyle, "I made ze look at ze Lady."

"O Bow Ling Ali," replied the Camel Pilot, "Shaykh of the Children of Hi Bal, All-wise Defender of the Prophet, this unclean son of the west gazed with Profane Eyes upon the features of Little Egypt."

"Hold!" said the Shaykh; "this being an

affair of the heart, it shall be settled after the Usual Fashion.''

Thereupon the Spectators made a Squared Circle and, in the absence of Malachi Hogan, Shaykh All-wise acted as Referee.

The Arab made a Snakelike spring and Collided with M. Broyle's famous left foot, while the Stranger's Right Foot beat a gentle Tattoo on his Metric System.

After the Parisian had walked around the Arab's face until it looked like the Home Plate, the police interfered.

Now, it is not necessary to state whether the Camel Pilot recovered or whether M. Broyle, savate expert, at your service, won the Fair Damsel or no. This Fable really concerns mostly a man who appeared on the scene three days after the Savate demonstration, and who knew nothing about it.

This stranger was a River Driver from Cloquet. He was on a Pedestrian Tour of the World. He wore his Spiked Boots, size 11½, not only because they were Comfortable, but because the sand could not then burn his feet.

Now, when the man with the 11½ Spiked Boots approached the village of Hi Bal the scouts of Shaykh Bow Ling Ali discovered his Foot Prints and carried the awful intelligence to the All-wise. When the river driver appeared in Person he beheld only a Cloud of Dust in the Distance.

He wondered thereat; but he picked the best of the remaining Horses and proceeded on his Journey.

Moral—We cowards often Unconsciously Owe a good deal to some Other Fellow who has passed this Way.

Of the Three Sons Who Were Put to the Arabian Test

A certain Lumberman, who owned a saw mill in the Land where the Big Timber blossoms with Red Cedar Shingles, had Three Ambitions in Life—all of them Boys. In fact he had about all the Ambition that appeared to run in the Family.

Not but what these were Active boys. One of them held the Driving Record on four different Links and could make Eighteen Holes in 61. Another had broken a Red Devil Wagon so he could bring it up to the Curb at thirty miles an hour and it would stand Without hitching. The other was gone on a Girl on the North Side and was Gone most of the time.

None of these Three Great Responsibilities had yet, however, evinced any Desire for Work. They were Shining Examples of the doctrine, "What's the Use of Working while Father keeps his Health?" This was a Question they had never been able to Solve; so they let it go at that. It never occurred to the Boy with the Knee Pants and Sassy Hose to use his Niblick to shift a belt in the saw mill. The lad who tooted the Comanche business on the front end of the Juggernaut did not know Anything about a sawmill engine, and if asked what the Governor was would have said it was the Old Guy who Paid the Bills. The boy who was Stuck on the North Side Dame never worried about where his Wedding Outfit was coming from. He knew Dad was good for a Gas Stove and a Wilton Rug, or at least could Furnish Five Rooms for $87.

None of the boys ever thought any Further Ahead than the Thursday night Hop or any Further Back than 2 o'clock this morning. But the Old Man Used to meet Himself in the Study some nights and wonder if Those Boys were ever going to awaken to the Seriousness of Life or whether he would have to set off the Alarm.

About this time Dad got hold of a book called "The Shaykh of the Desert." He did not know whether "Shaykh" was the name of a Grade or a What. But he thought he would find out.

So he read the book. It appears that this Shaykh was the Main Squeeze of an Arabian Village and used to Hand Out large Gobs of Wisdom to the Wondering Natives. He was a Regular Detective, except that he really Detected Crime. His favorite method was to put the Suspected Person to a test—such as Twisting the Tail of a White Mule. If the mule kicked the Respondent in the Experiment or the Chest or Somewhere it was an indication that the Respondent was innocent. It was also sometimes accompanied by Indications that the Respondent was Dead.

The name of this Shaykh was Bow Ling Ali, and he Worked up such a Rep for being a Wise Member that one of the Met Saleys of the tribe picked up a bushel basket full of his Wise Thinks and Coagulated them in a Book, which might be had for $3.50 and in State Street for $1.98. It was a copy of the $1.98 Edition that fell into the hands of the Lumberman, and that gave him an Idee. He had Suspicions that perhaps One of the Boys might be Concealing Brains about his Person somewhere, but Concealing them with a Success worthy of a Better Cause. He decided to do a little Shaykh business Himself and put the Boys to the Arabian Test. But he was undetermined how to put them over the Hot sands, as he possessed no White Mule.

After some Cogitation he called the Three Candidates before him and Handed each a Round Trip Ticket to the World's Fair, together with a suitable Sum of Coin. He then addressed them in the Language of the Desert:

"You Three Skalawags may think your Pa is a Pudding; but if you do you are off your Cafe Noir, whatever that is. It is about time that you, Harold, quit carrying around that bundle of Children's Garden Tools and got busy driving a Dump-Cart instead of a Golf Ball. And you, Bob, if you want to commit murder, do not need to kill off pedestrians, but can blow up a few sawmill Boilers. And, Harry, Love is a Good Thing to live on if it is placed between two Slices of Bread and Spread thickly with minced Ham and Mustard.

"Now you Three Galoots have got to go to Work or to a Home for the Feeble Minded. I am going to send you down to this World's Fair and see what you can Learn. After you come back, and pass through a little Uncivil Service Examination I intend giving you, I will start you out in Life according to the Wisdom you have Assimilated. Now, Bless you, my Children; and if you Walk Crooked you know what you will Get when you Come Back."

Thereupon the Three Sons set out across the Plains until they came to the Great City. There they saw Many Sights; for there were Quite a Few to be seen.

When they Returned to the Land of their Fathers the Old Man said, "Come with me." He took them first through Devious Ways, where there was Music and Dancing, and he asked them what they Beheld. Bob and Harry knew not; but Harold told him it was the Pasmala.

Then he Steered them to a Place where there were Picture Cards and Buttons with no Holes in them. He pointed to a table and asked, "What is this?" Harold and Harry knew not; but Bob opined it was Three Card Monte.

Next he took them to a Place where Trees cut in Thin Slices were stood on end. He pointed to a Slice that was as beautiful as a Sunset. Bob and Harold were up a stump; but Harry said it was Red Gum.

Thereupon the disciple of Bow Ling Ali was content. And the next morning he arose and gave Harry $87 to furnish five rooms, and a Lumber Yard to furnish the Grub. But to Harold he presented a Swift Kick, and gave Bob a job pushing a Cart in Harry's Yard.

Moral—There is a whole lot of Cull in the Tree of Knowledge.

Of the Reformer Reformed

Once upon a Good Old Summer Time there was a Reformer who was a Glittering Success. A Reformer is a Chap who is so Busy keeping Cases on other people's Faults that he has no Time to Post his Own Books. It's a Job that will keep a man fairly busy; and the other Fellow who runs out ahead to give the Millennium the Glad Hand is apt to get out of Breath before he has to make his Speech of Welcome. The Optimist who is Wandering around looking for a State of Perfection is likely to discover that it has not yet been Admitted to the Union—though New York may try to convince him that it is It.

This particular Reformer was doing an Anti-Trust Specialty. He was agin the Trusts; and the directors of the Steel Trust used to Sit up Nights worrying about it. It never Occurred to them to buy him off with a few Shares of Steel Stock, though He often Thought of it. He used to Discourse on Great Aggravations of Capital and all that kind of thing. He used to Orate about the Lumber Trust; though, when it came to a Showdown, he could never lay his Hand on it. Finally he Stumbled on the Health Food Trust.

He Discovered that all the Breakfast Food Builders had formed a Combination that made the Combination on the vault door of the First National Bank in Chicago look as easy as a Prize Rebus in a Piano ad. This Trust he Viewed with Alarm. He saw Starvation Staring People in the Face if their Breakfast Food was cornered.

Now it also came to Pass that at about the same time the Anti-Trust business was not yielding very heavy Dividends. It was Very Disappointing to go forth and stir the Hearts of the Multitude on the Dangers of Capitalistic Encroachment and then have only 89 cents in the Collection. So, while he went about Discussing the Trusts, he took up Inventing as a Side Line.

It was while he was belaboring the Health Food Trust at Night and Working on a Model of a Flying Machine by Day that he discovered a Perfect Substitute for Oats and Barley in the Manufacture of Breakfast Food. He began Experimenting, interested Capital—that Villain Capital!—built a Factory and put the Health Food Trust on the Bum in a Year with Competition when he Couldn't have more than made it wiggle its tail with a Century of Wind Jamming. Everybody switched off from the Regular

Health Foods to the Substitute. The Inventor kept the Secret of the Invention to himself.

Then one Morning the World awoke with a Headache to find that a Sawdust Trust had been Formed during the Night. The Wise Inventor had kept the Process by which the Substitute was manufactured a Secret until he had Cornered all the Sawdust in the World.

Thus Fell the Reformer; but his wife now gets $2,158,976 a Month for Pin Money.

Moral — No Game looks Wicked after You Butt in.

Of Telling You So

Once there lived Side by Side two little boys. Because the back doors of their Homes looked at Each other, it must not be supposed that their people Mixed to any Considerable extent. The lads Mixed it in the Alley once in a while, but that was the Extent of the Social Intercourse between the neighbors. The difficulty was the fact that Harold was the Son of a Saw Mill owner who lived on Front street, while Sammy was the Son of a Dump Cart driver who lived on Back street.

As the Boys grew up there wasn't a Wish that

Harold did not have Gratified, except the Desire to win One of those alley Encounters; as for Sammy, these Three-round Affairs in the alley were the only Fun he had. Sammy learned to Depend on Himself for what he Got; Harold Drew on the Old Man.

At about the time they both became old enough to Vote, the Saw Mill man moved Out West, because he was Cleaning up only Ten Thousand a year in the Old Town; and Sammy's father went along to work for him, because he Always Had. The Years went by, according to Schedule. Then News came that each of the boys had Received a Term in Colorado. Sammy's was in the Legislature at Denver; Harold's was in the Pen at Canon City.

Then the Wise Guys in the old town Held a mutual admiration meeting. There was not a Man or Woman in the Burg that did not Know all the time that those two boys would Turn Out that way, and the I-told-you-so Fiend went Up and Down the Pike challenging Successful Contradiction. It was a beautiful Opportunity to Hand it to the Sons of the Rich.

One would naturally think that the Wiseacres would have felt something of a Jar when word came six months Later that it had been Discovered that Harold was Falsely Accused and that Sammy had been Stuffing ballot-boxes at Orchard Place. But you have another Think coming. The Mutual Admiration Society in the Old Town Reconvened and Agreed that it knew all the time that Blood would Tell.

Moral—Many people would rather be Inconsistent than Mistaken; in consequence they are Both.

Of the Man Who Was Troubled With Insomnia

Once upon a time there was a man who was Troubled with Insomnia and a Saw mill. He complained to the Bookkeeper about the Insomnia, and the bookkeeper advised him to have it Lanced. Of course the Bookkeeper didn't know what Insomnia is. The Bookkeeper could sleep as Hearty as a Babe. A good Tough Trial Balance would send him off into a Rip Van Winkle that, by Comparison, made a Chicago policeman look as active as a Campaign lie.

The Mill man's friends suggested Remedies that varied all the way from Morphine to Huntereye. None of these medicaments ever did him good, although several professional

Experimenters did—and Plenty. The Sawmill man came in time to Brag that there wasn't a thing in the Heavyweight class that could Put him to sleep—not even Al Kaufman or the Congressional Record.

About this time he casually met a William Goat in the alley, head-on, and a humble he-sheep did what Medical Science and the Congressional flapdoodle had failed to accomplish. Kind neighbors found him, after remarking it was a Shame he Drank, carried him into the woodshed, and sent for the Village Pain-knocker and Billbooster. The Disciple of Galen Explored him about five Moments and announced that no bones were broken, but that the Snooze looked good for a week or Eight Days. Then they Locked up the Goater and put the Goatee to bed and Hired a Tame Nurse to keep People and Flies out of the Room at $20 per.

Meanwhile the Insomnia patient had a Beautiful Dream. It made the ordinary Pipe-Siesta look like a Boarding House Vision. He dreamed that the Theory of Transmigration had come to pass and that he had been Bunted into the Middle of a Future Existence. He was in another World.

Finally he wandered up-street and came to what he Presumed was a Department Store— one of those places where you give up Good

Money for the Privilege of being Walked on by fat Women looking for the Peau d'Soie. But he had another Presume coming, for when he approached yet more nearer his eye fell on a sign which read:

"SPHERES EXCHANGED."

This aroused the Dreamer's curiosity. He butted in. He found the place thronged with a Great Throng of ex-persons like himself. Of course, most of the others had come in on Regular Trains and not on the Billy Goat Express. Nevertheless, they were there.

The man who had arrived on the Sheep Special finally discovered that this was the place where People came to have their Spheres in life refitted. On earth some of them had occupied Spheres that fitted them about as well as A. Scalper would adorn the Presidency of the National Wholesale Lumber Dealers' Association.

A floor-walker explained it to the Earthly one. "Y' see," said the Gentlemanly Usher, "every Gazabo who breaks into Utopia (this is the place) is backed up to a looking-glass to see how his Sphere fits. If he has been Blundering Along down Below, undoing something that he ought not to have been doing in the First place, or this place, we take it away from him and give him Something that will make him Self-supporting."

"You say 'him'," remarked the man with the lovely snooze on. "Are there no women up here, yes?"

"The other seventeen Floors are the Women's Departments," replied the Official Guyed, assuming a more Troubled air. "The women keep us exercised more than the men; but we have effected some Marvelous Cures which are verified by Testimonials from Thankful Patients now on file in this office."

"The patients?"

"No, the Testimonials. There is, for instance, the Chairwoman of the Committee to Give Advice to the Czar, of the Binglewood Woman's Club. Why, when that Woman Invaded this place she even said she was Chair*man* of that Committee! Now she is the head of a Happy Home and has actually made the Acquaintance of her Children. The President of the Young Ladies' Floral Association for Condemned Murderers now sends her Bouquets to the Sick."

The Somnolent Sawmiller had come to the Conclusion (this Tale is far from that) that Utopia was almost as good a place as the South Side.

"How about the Brutes?" he asked, pointing to the Gentlemen's Furnishing Department, where new Spheres were being Passed out like watermelon at a Newsboys' Picnic.

"See that Sign-painter there?" asked the Steering Gear. "He used to hang around the Art Institute. Observe the Gazabo in the Salt Department? On the earth he thought he was a Sash and Door salesman. Now he is a Salt Seller. That fellow with the long Hair, the Hatchet Face and orang-outang arms thought he was a Poet. He is Carrying a Hod up here. This man to the left was a Reporter; now he is a Sampler in a Distillery. An ex-teamster is now a Boss over Men; he was too cruel to handle Mules. This statue of Cupid was a Messenger Boy. No, he was not made into a Cupid because he loved to Work; but we put the Speed Indicator on him and found he was better suited for Statuary." .

The Sawmill man butted into the remarks again. "As for myself," said he, "I used to be a Lumberman. I am a little curious to know about That Business. Any Lumbermen up here?"

"Lots of People," said the Guyed, "who Think they are Lumbermen come up here. Of course, no one ever told them they were. We have a Sawmill man who is running a Sausage machine and making a Success."

"Don't you ever Make a Mistake?"

"Once in a While. We put one of those anti-

Association Retailers at work running a Peanut Stand, but he made a Failure of it."

"Everybody up here seems to Break Out of the lumber Business. Don't anybody ever Break into the Lumber Business up here?"

"Of course not—this is Heaven."

"Don't anybody ever come up Here who is the Right Man in the Right Place?"

"Oh, yes. There was, for Instance, the Alderman who came up here in a Cage."

At this juncture the floor-walker took on a bizzy-izzy manner. "However," he said, briskly, "this is our Busy Day. We have just received a Batch of folks who Learned Journalism by means of a Three Weeks Correspondence Course, and we've got to get them back to Laundry Work. So your case 'll be next. You are a Sawmill Man?"

"Yes."

"What are your Symptoms?"

The Sawmill Man described how he sat up with himself every night.

"You say you have no Desire to Sleep?"

"That's it."

The Inspector called an Assistant. "Take this man," he said, "and get him a job as a Night Watchman. That 'll cure him."

Moral—Is your Sphere on Straight?

Of the Man Who Wanted to Borrow Money

A Lumberman who was entitled to the Title because he had Lumbered for twenty Years and pretty well learned every Department of the Industry, from Chopping the Tree to Working up Common into A1 sash, became inoculated with the Idea that he would like to go into Business for himself. He knew the Lumber Trade from Alpha to Omega and from Boston, Mass., to Hope, Ida. He had skidded Logs, tail-sawed, piled and even sold a little Lumber for someone Else; and so the idea that he would like to be his own Boss came naturally. He was not the first young Lumberman who had got such a Bee in his Bonnet.

He dreamed about it with a Constancy that even his wife's mince pie could not Interrupt. However, though he had Dreamed about it with such devoted Regularity, he had not saved up very much Coin against the day when he should wish to launch forth upon the Business Sea. For some Years during the early part of his lumbering Career he had put his shoulder to the Family Wheel, so his early Training and hard Knocks brought him no Profit but Experience.

Now, Experience is a Good Thing, but a Poor one on which to negotiate a Loan.

After he had helped to start Sundry Small Brothers on successful Careers, so successful, in fact, that they came to look upon their Big Brother with Condescension and to avoid Reference to the Relationship in Conversation with Others, he did another Expensive thing. He Fell in Love. This was a Wise thing to do. He drew a Prize in the Marriage Lottery who Cheered his Despondency and Made his Socks last Two Summers. His Marriage was followed by the Usual Consequences—six of them. The Young Lumberman did not object to this. But they all took Money. In consequence, when the Opportunity to break into the Lumber Business presented itself, it found the young lumberman, as the after-dinner speakers say, "totally unprepared."

The Opportunity came rather Suddenly. The Opportunities of a Poor man Generally do, and they do not Linger long. It seems that another young man more fortunately situated Financially had been set up in the Retail Lumber business in our Hero's town. This other Youth was a good fellow, but he Lacked Experience with Lumber and People. In consequence the yard was not a Howling Success. Instead, it was a quite Audible Failure. It didn't get the

120 RESAWED FABLES

Business that the Stock warranted. The local Banks thought the Yard was to blame. Our Hero knew where the trouble lay. Finally the Yard man got Tired, and the people who were Behind him became somewhat Fatigued themselves. Then it went out that the yard was For Sale.

Here was our Hero's opportunity. He had no capital. But he had his fellow-townsmen with him, he had Experience, and he had "a Way about him." In fact, he had everything that Makes for Success except Money. He was doomed to learn that he lacked the Principal Ingredient. He struck a bargain with the Yard Man first. Then he went out to borrow the Money.

He went to the Banks, but had no Security to Offer but a Firm Conviction that he would Succeed. There was Nothing Doing. He became Despondent. His Good Wife cheered his Despondency, but that was all she could do; it was his Shoes that he wore out now.

Next he went to Men of Means, but they were Equally Timid. They all Declared they were on the Brink of Financial Ruin. He did not blame them Much, but he wished they had as much Confidence in him as his Wife had. At last, as a Last Resort, he went to the People he should have gone to First. He went to the people who had already sunk some Thousands in the Yard. They saw the Difference. He pulled them out Better than Even, and did better than that for Himself.

Moral—A man never realizes how Poor he is until he needs Money; and he never realizes how poor Other People are until he tries to Borrow it.

Of the Model Young Man and the Jobs That Lingered Not

A certain gazabo had been selling lumber and the Retail Trade for Ten Years without ever amassing a Batting Average that seemed to entitle him to Break into Faster Company. As a matter of Fact he was playing the Bench most of the time; and when he did Catch On his salary indicated that he was hitting them out at about .178, whereas he considered himself a .343 Swatter and that he had Larry Lajoie and Sam Crawford beaten a City Block. Having just said Farewell to his last Job, and being anxious to Catch the Drag to Prosperity, he anchored himself to a Park Seat and tried to reason the matter out—a very reckless Thing for him to attempt.

Personally he considered himself one of the

Best that ever came down the Pike. He did not have the Swelled Head so much, however, that he could not sit up and Recognize the fact that other Funny Folks thought he was a Shine and a Skate. This led him to wonder what was the Matter with Hannah. He had held good Jobs, but he had been canned so often that he felt like the Pickled Peaches that Mother used to make. In fact, it seemed that every Time he made his Getaway he left behind him the faintly audible rattle of Tin. His whole life seemed to consist of being chased away from good Jobs. Everywhere, at the end of two Weeks it was the glassy Eye and the Marble Heart and "Here's your Hat—what's your Hurry?" He would no more than Tack onto what looked like a good Proposition than he would get a Hunch that a Vacancy in his Department would be much appreciated.

He had become so Accustomed to the Sidetracking Stunt that he half expected that one of the Cops would spy him on the Park seat and tell him to Hike along. But there was not a Copper in sight, and the man out of Luck was permitted to Soliloquize on the Why there was no Cush in his kick.

Like a Chesty Willie, he sized up first the places where he was the Strong Man from Akron. He whispered to himself the fact, for instance, that he was not a Booze Fighter. He had been on the Water Wagon ten years and could Wave away a Manhattan without the Quiver of an Eyelid. He knew nothing about Hop Joints, and his life was one of Moral Rectitude. In spite of being on his Uppers, he never Piped it off in his Raiment; for he wore Glad Rags seven days in the week and Sported a Watch Fob big enough for Balloon Ballast. At the Jollying Game he had a line of Hot Air second to None, and could untie a wheeze or hold up his end of a Talkfest like a Tonsorial Impresario. He used to hang around lumber Offices for hours talking about Himself, because he thought it would Please the Children.

But he didn't sell any Lumber, which was a Sad and Bitter Disappointment. The House invariably shared in this Disappointment and left him reading that thrilling romance, "Male Help Wanted."

Our Hero at the time our Story opens was engaged in Warming a Seat in the Park and trying to locate the Cause of the whole Trouble. Needless to say, he's there yet. Here's the Answer:

Moral—To be Popular, avoid being Autobiographical. Talk about the Other Fellow; or, if you can't, let Him do it.

Of the Uses of Experience

L. M. Knotz and his son C. Dar Knotz differed slightly on the Question of Football. The Difference was about as Slight as that between a Shipper and a Buyer in the Grading of a Car of lumber. C. Dar Knotz thought that Football was great Sport and a necessary Part of a College Education; L. M. Knotz thought that it was great Sport for the Hero on top of the Heap, but (a Place which it might not be well to mention) for the Gazabo with the Ball, who was at the Bottom. As for being a necessary and Component Part of a Higher Education, L. M. Knotz thought that that depended to some considerable Degree on the Circumstances. If the Student was going to be a Divine, or a Corporation Lawyer, Knotz the Elder could not see that a Football Education was Essential. A man might not be able to handle Punts, and still be able to preach a Passable Sermon. He might not know much about Breaking up Interference, and still be able to Fracture a Fat Will. Of course, if the Student intended to be a Bowery Policeman, or had to ride Home every night on one of the suburbans, a Graduation from the Gridiron might help Some.

L. M. Knotz had other Plans for his Son and Heir, however. He had not mapped out a

Brilliant Career in the Pulpit for him, partly because C. Dar Knotz had not Exhibited any Desire to Leap into a Pastorate Immediately upon leaving the Brain Factory. Neither did L. M. Knotz anticipate making a Lawyer out of the boy—in fact, he was Laboring to keep the boy as far from the Bar as possible. His fond Parental heart figured that "L. M. Knotz & Son" would look a good deal better on the Glass Door than just "L. M. Knotz, Wholesale Lumber," as at Present. The younger Knotz had as yet not decided the matter for Father. He didn't care to Row with the Old Man about the Lumber Business; but he was compelled to differ with him on the Football Proposition. The Football Question looks Different from the Halfback position than it does from the Sidelines. It was Natural, however, that L. M. Knotz and his great responsibility, C. Dar Knotz, should Differ on the Football Question. Football looks different to the man who can hardly run One yard and to a man who can Run a Hundred yards in :10 flat.

When C. Dar Knotz joined the Football squad, Knotz, Sr., was dubious. When Coach Yost transferred him to the 'Varsity team, Knotz, Jr., went into Raptures and his Father into Convulsions. Knotz, Sr., is a Bum Penman, but the Epistle he indited to Knotz, Jr., was very

Plain. It was so Plain that he who Ran might Read—in fact, so Plain and to the Point that he who Read might Run.

But Knotz, Jr., didn't Run. He wrote a long Collect Telegram to Father in which he said Things about the Glory of the School and how he ought to want his Son to be a Credit to his Alma Mater. Football, he declared, was a Harmless Amusement, and he asked Father to come down and see a Game, just to Satisfy himself. As Knotz, Sr., had been Coming Down for Knotz, Jr., ever since the boy learned the way to the Candy Store, he didn't know why he should not come down now. So he came Down.

Any Football Player will tell you that it always works that Way. A man may go through a Season without a Scratch; but let him Invite some Fond One down to a game to Prove that Football is simply Scientific Tag, and he will be reduced to Pulp in the First Scrimmage. On the Day Appointed, L. M. Knotz was in a Front Seat in the Bleachers. He saw C. Dar out on the Field with a Uniform on that looked like the Czar's Bullet-proof Nightshirt. The Game started. L. M. Knotz, Respectable Wholesale Lumber Dealer, felt rather Foolish at first. But when he saw a Bald-headed man, with eight Yards of Ribbon on his coat and no Hat on, Two-stepping on a 6 x 4 plank seat 40 feet above the Ground, he decided there were still a few others Loose.

Then Pennsylvania fumbled, and a little chap on C. Dar's side yelled "4—11—44." He saw C. Dar grab a brown Watermelon and Butt in. Another fellow was so delighted to see him that he Rushed up and Embraced him. When about twenty others, the best that Knotz, Sr., could Estimate, rushed up to shake hands with C. Dar, Knotz, Sr., swelled with pride. Play Football? Well, he guessed he could—all he wanted to. Knotz, Sr., had no idea the boy was so Popular. But the Pennsylvania man, whose name they said was Ike, but who didn't look the Part, had embraced C. Dar so hard they Both fell down and the rest all stumbled on top of them.

When they got up again, C. Dar didn't get up. They carried him off the Field, and when Knotz, Sr., looked at him he wondered how C. Dar's friend Ike, of Pennsylvania, had recognized him. Incidentally, Michigan lost a Football Star. "Parental Objection," the sporting editors said. But a Compromise was effected. Knotz, Jr., was to play Football in college; then he was to enter the Lumber Business, if he survived.

He never got another Bruise. After graduation he started to learn the lumber business. Knotz, Sr., believed in beginning at the Bottom. C. Dar began by Piling Lumber. One day he and a man of unknown Nationality, whose name was Ole Olson, were piling 3 x 8s. There came a burst of thunder Sound, and Knotz, Sr., and Everybody within a Mile rushed to the spot. They sent Olson home in a Gunnysack. Then they began looking for young Knotz.

Finally a lumber-shover beheld a Leg. They removed a few more 3 x 8s, and then the lumber-shover Pulled the Leg respectfully. C. Dar Knotz staggered to his feet.

"What down is this?" he asked.

Moral—The Value of Experience lies not so much in the Success we Achieve as in the Calamity we Avoid.

BIBLIOLIFE

Old Books Deserve a New Life
www.bibliolife.com

Did you know that you can get most of our titles in our trademark **EasyScript**™ print format? **EasyScript**™ provides readers with a larger than average typeface, for a reading experience that's easier on the eyes.

Did you know that we have an ever-growing collection of books in many languages?

Order online:
www.bibliolife.com/store

Or to exclusively browse our **EasyScript**™ collection:
www.bibliogrande.com

At BiblioLife, we aim to make knowledge more accessible by making thousands of titles available to you – quickly and affordably.

Contact us:
BiblioLife
PO Box 21206
Charleston, SC 29413

CPSIA information can be obtained at www.ICGtesting.com
Printed in the USA
LVOW13s2344270414

383446LV00025B/990/P